CHOOSING HOPE

CHOOSING
HOPE

1 Woman. 3 Cancers.

A STORY OF INSPIRATION, RESILIENCE AND COURAGE

Munira Premji

MAWEN ZI
HOUSE

We acknowledge the support of the Canada Council for the Arts for our publishing program. We also acknowledge support from the Government of Ontario through the Ontario Arts Council.

Library and Archives Canada Cataloguing in Publication

Title: Choosing hope : 1 woman, 3 cancers : a story of inspiration, resilience and courage / Munira Premji.
Names: Premji, Munira, 1959- author.
Identifiers: Canadiana (print) 20200178032 | Canadiana (ebook) 20200178040 | ISBN 9781774150054 (softcover) | ISBN 9781774150061 (HTML) | ISBN 9781774150078 (PDF)
Subjects: LCSH: Premji, Munira, 1959-—Health. | LCSH: Cancer—Patients—Canada— Biography. | LCSH:
Cancer—Psychological aspects. | LCGFT: Autobiographies.
Classification: LCC RC265.6.P74 A3 2020 | DDC 362.19699/40092—dc23

The "popular saying" on p 145 is often referred to as an "Eskimo Proverb," but we have not been able to acknowledge a source.

Printed and bound in Canada by Coach House Printing

Mawenzi House Publishers Ltd.
39 Woburn Avenue (B)
Toronto, Ontario M5M 1K5
Canada

www.mawenzihouse.com

To Nagib, my husband, the love of my life.

To Shayne, my son, my inspirer and encourager.

To Sabrina, my daughter and my best friend in the whole wide expanding universe, for lovingly infusing each page with feeling and meaning, re-living difficult parts of the journey each time she worked on the book.

To Zera, my mom, my anchor and role model.

To Drs Tiedemann, Pinchuk, Robson, Franke, Baghdadlian, Cserti, and all the health professionals who everyday deal in the vicissitudes of life, hope, and death.

To people battling cancer, and to those who have succumbed to the illness.

To the caregivers of cancer patients because you can't do cancer alone.

I am proud to be represented by Mawenzi House, who believed that my story was worth telling and for bringing this memoir to life. Special thanks to Nurjehan Aziz, the publisher, and MG Vassanji, my brilliant editor, for his partnership and collaboration.

Foreword

As a hematologist and scientist working at a prestigious cancer center, caring for cancer patients, I am often led to wonder how I would respond if one day I or a loved one was on the receiving end of a major cancer diagnosis. After hearing the words "you have cancer" and becoming lost in the disorienting fog that may materialize around a cancer diagnosis, how does one prevail to find the inner peace and resolution to forge a new path ahead, over which only partial control may be possible? Munira's story, and that of her family, is both confronting and inspirational. Diagnosed not with one but initially with two and eventually, devastatingly, with three advanced cancers, she makes the simple but profound decision to choose hope.

To know Munira is to love her. And her family. Self-identifying as a "Type A" personality, she is a miraculous mix of energy and humility, spiced with a contagious zest for life and a selfless willingness to lift up and empower others.

In February 2012, after meeting Munira in the outpatient clinic for the first time, shortly after she became unwell, I judged with a certain skepticism her pathology report describing in professionally understated phrases the presence of two simultaneous new cancers, multiple myeloma and large B-cell lymphoma, occupying her bone marrow. Not one, but two cancers. Presenting at the same time and in the same place. Competing to outgrow one another like primeval beasts.

Given the serious implications of a diagnosis with either of these cancers, and recognizing the possibility of human error, the first rec-ommendation that I made to Munira and her husband, Nagib, was that we repeat the bone marrow test to check whether there had been some sort of mistake. I recommended this despite the pain that a second biopsy would cause. Alas, the repeat biopsy quickly returned the same result: two cancers, conquering distinct geographical zones within her marrow. There was no easy escape from this reality.

With two aggressive malignancies invading her bone marrow, the biological "factory" where blood is made, Munira soon fell criti-cally ill. Before she could even start treatment, her red blood counts had dropped precipitously from coincident hammer blows of failing bone marrow function, immune red cell destruction, and thalassemia. Within weeks emergent fungal and viral infections revealed an immune system that was overwhelmed and struggling. Munira found herself fighting for her life even before the battle to conquer her cancers had begun.

Much later, after many months of chemotherapy and an autolo-gous hematopoietic stem-cell transplant, there was remission. And the chance for healing. And then, unjustly, a new cancer stole forth. In shock and disbelief at first, but with growing determination and fight-ing spirit, this too was faced with steadfast hope and beaten back.

There is an inexplicable unfairness in any cancer diagnosis. Unlike other maladies that assail mankind, the pathos of cancer is the transfor-mation of self into assailant. For a disease of such terrorizing impact, its beginnings, in painful contrast, are crushingly trivial. The origins of cancer almost invariably lie in a momentary molecular mistake, strik-ing deep within a single cell: microscopic ephemeral events that ini-tially are so trivial that in the passing of the hour they uniformly go undetected, unrecognized. Yet years later, when those first elemental errors have burgeoned into full-blown cancer, the universal question inevitably arises: Why? To which no answer is quite so universal.

Enduring three cancers is beyond unfair. Yet despite the agonies inherent to such a chronicle, the story recounted here by Munira, her husband Nagib, and their grown children, Shayne and Sabrina, is in the end an empowering tale of courage, optimism, survival, and triumph. This is not a story they envisaged for themselves. Yet from a real world calamity they bring forth a remarkable tale of hope and endurance.

As a medical student and junior doctor, I learned the possibilities of the medical treatment of cancer, imperfect as this is. I also heard whispered the importance of hope. However, it was only through meeting Munira and sharing her cancer journey that I learned the true power of hope. In the conflict with cancer, hope is at the epicenter. Hope is a choice. And the freedom to choose hope is a personal prerogative. These are precious lessons for which I take no credit. For these powerful revelations, to Munira, and to the many other remarkable individuals who have taught and inspired me as they waged their personal battles with cancer, I stand forever indebted to you.

Once caught in the swirling fog of cancer, when the path ahead is narrow and reservations abound, is it reasonable to find comfort and sustenance in Hope?

Unquestionably, unreservedly, yes.

Dr Rodger F. Tiedemann MB, ChB, PhD, FRACP, FRCPA
Associate Professor of Medicine, University of Toronto
Hematologist and Senior Scientist,
Princess Margaret Cancer Centre, Toronto

My Journey

My name is Munira Premji. On February 3, 2012, life as I knew it stopped suddenly. I was in the emergency ward at Toronto General Hospital. Over the past couple of months my hemoglobin count had been dropping steadily and I was drained. While in emergency overnight, I was poked and prodded for blood and then, the following morning, I underwent a painful bone-marrow biopsy as the doctors tried to figure out what was going on inside me. I was admitted into the hospital under the care of Dr Robert Wu, a gentle, unassuming internal medicine doctor in his early 40s. Later that day, after an excruciating wait, I saw Dr Wu pace by my room a few times, and I sensed that he wanted to speak to us but something was holding him back. Finally, after about twenty minutes, he came into the room, rubbed his eyes, sat down on the chair beside my hospital bed and looked at my husband Nagib and me for what seemed like an eternity. He took my hands in his and said quietly, "You have multiple myeloma, an incurable cancer of the blood." In that one moment, our world changed. It became binary, divided thenceforth into before and after. We were broken. We felt our lives had been destroyed; we didn't know what to do. The words "cancer" and "incurable" echoed in our minds. I felt trapped in an intermediate space between life and death.

While we were still grappling with this news, back at home and at work, Dr Jean Wang, a hematologist I had met while I was in emergency, called me the following week to say, "You need to come back to the hospital. Your bone marrow is showing abnormal activity and we need to run more tests."

Nothing could have prepared me for the results. A second cancer: Stage 4, non-Hodgkin lymphoma.

Within a six-week period, I went from thinking I was perfectly healthy to finding out that I had two different cancers, both in their advanced stages. But this was not the end of my relationship with the disease. Four years later, in 2015, after successfully recovering from lymphoma and putting myeloma into remission, I was diagnosed with yet another cancer, this time Stage 3 breast cancer. Each diagnosis has had a profound impact on my life and the lives of my family.

It was my daughter Sabrina who originally suggested that I write a blog to keep family and friends informed about my journey with cancer. After many hours of friendly banter, we landed on the name of the blog: www.i-will-survive.org and I began writing my entries in March 2012. The blog started simply as a venue where I could pour out my thoughts and share my stories of life on the cancer train—the good and the not-so-good parts. It meant showing myself to others without holding back for fear of rejection and judgement. Being vulnerable was difficult for me. I was accustomed to sharing only what I wanted others to see or know about me, usually the shiny, pretty, and fun stuff. This blog challenged me to share the deepest parts of my heart and mind.

Over time the readership of the blog grew to some 200,000 hits with people from 80 countries. Readers started to comment on the posts and share advice and prayers. The blog became more than just my own personal journal. I made new friends and reconnected with old ones whom I had not seen in decades. In the early days, when I spent so much time in the hospital and was too sick to go out, the blog became my salvation, my way to be part of the rhythm of life.

There were times when I didn't have much to say or didn't feel like writing. Soon I would get phone calls and emails from people asking if I was okay. Many worried that the absence of a blog post meant that my life had come to an abrupt end. Their encouragement gave me the confidence to continue to blog. When a few friends suggested I write a book, in the spirit of living fearlessly I decided to do just that.

I had been headed in a predictable, normal direction until the cancers invaded my life one after another and hit me so hard that I could never look back. Some days I feel like I have lived with cancer for a very long time; other days, it feels like I was only diagnosed yesterday. It was only when I surrendered completely and utterly to my new reality, stopped fighting it and accepted the new direction my life had taken that I found peace and strength.

I discovered new goals, new interests, a new purpose. I have become more human, more patient, more loving. For all the pain that I have suffered, I have found that the disease has brought me so much more. It has made me more aware and appreciative of the richness and texture of life and the gifts it offers. It has been a transformational experience for my family as well who were going through their own journeys and reflections.

This book is a story of self-discovery, learning, and reinvention. My goal here is to share my insights from my experiences with cancer. Each new diagnosis came with new lessons to learn.

Stage 4 non-Hodgkin lymphoma taught me how to take a devastating diagnosis and find a way through it with the support of family. It thrust me into the unfamiliar territory of the world of cancer —the health care system, the services that are available, and the necessity of patient advocacy. It was a time of heartbreaking losses—losses of identity, independence, and confidence—as I saw first-hand what it was like to live as a cancer patient and experienced the horrible side-effects of treatment. Earlier, while I was still in diagnosis, before I could even start treatment, I almost died when my hemoglobin dropped so low that there was fear that every organ in my body would shut down. In those moments I understood deeply the fragility of life and the need to make the most of every second we are blessed with.

As I was going through treatment for multiple myeloma, I learned about the fascinating world of stem-cell transplants and the importance of research and funding to find the causes and cures for cancer. I also joined the Multiple Myeloma Support Group in Toronto, which connected me to other sufferers and caregivers and provided a forum for education, discussion, and encouragement. As I was starting to feel better, my son, Shayne, encouraged me to make a movie of my experiences. I was on a high dose of steroids at that time and I used the manic energy that is a side effect of these drugs to pour myself into the project. With the help of my friend Frances Darwin we filmed a one-hour movie of my journey with cancer and shared this with almost 200 family members and friends at a movie theater in Toronto on the Thanksgiving weekend of 2013.

But it seemed that God was not done with me yet and had planned more lessons for me to learn. In December 2015, I was devastated to be diagnosed with breast cancer. While undergoing treatment for this, I made a commitment to work on my health and vitality, areas that I had largely ignored in the past. I started to work out, eat right and meditate, practices I have continued to today.

My relationship with cancer has been long, arduous, and painful, and yet also surprisingly positive. The adversity has been accompanied by generous amounts of optimism, blessings, and goodwill. I invite you to take this journey with me.

1.
DIAGNOSIS

My Life Before Cancer

I was born in Moshi, Tanzania, into an Ismaili Muslim family whose forefathers had migrated from the Indian subcontinent in the late 1800s and early 1900s. Moshi was famous for being on the foothills of Mount Kilimanjaro, the tallest mountain in Africa. Indeed, the word "moshi" is Swahili for "smoke," since a mist from the mountain would often envelope the town. As a child, I would jump out of bed, press my nose against the window and look at the majestic snow-covered peak. I would imagine climbing it to the very top. Our family was well-off and we lived a comfortable life. We had running water, a toilet inside the house and a much-envied television. At different times, my family owned a bakery, a coffee farm, a confectionery, a gas station, and a Pepsi-Cola bottling plant.

When I was fifteen, I attended the International School in Moshi, where I was exposed to people from all over the world, speaking every language imaginable. As I got to know students from Sweden, Finland, Denmark, the Philippines, Canada, and the United States, I could see that the world was far larger than my small town. Most of the students were from outside Moshi and lived in the school dormitory; they were close to each other and I often felt left out. I was one of the few students that lived at home and was dropped off to school every day. I was not confident, didn't think I was smart, didn't think I belonged. Hiding behind bell-bottom jeans and thick, black hair that fell to my hips, I tried to make myself invisible to my fellow students. Bea, a smart,

11

feisty, popular girl from the Philippines, and Patti, a kind, compassionate American, seemed to see past my insecurities. We spent recesses together, and I'd open up my world to them, inviting them home to have meals with my family. When I was eighteen, I was accepted into the only university in Tanzania, in Dar es Salaam, 274 miles away from home. My dad was uncomfortable about his daughter being away in the big city. Like many South Asian parents, he was overly protective and wanted to keep me at home for as long as possible. He proposed that I work with him in the family bakery and Pepsi-Cola factory as his executive assistant, and for two years, I did just that. I managed the banking, did some accounting, and sold bread at the counter. Most of our customers were retailers, who would sell individual loaves in their towns and villages. The aroma of warm, freshly baked bread still transports me back to this time.

My dad was a hard taskmaster. He expected perfection and was difficult to please. There were days when we would butt heads because we were both stubborn, with strong and differing opinions on most things. We had a tradition that I now look back on with fondness, although I resented it at the time. Every night at about nine o'clock, my mom, sister, and I would accompany my dad to the bakery and count the day's take for banking the next day. Once this was done, my dad would take a long, unhurried drive around town and ask me one single question: "What did you learn today?" One day I told him that I noticed that the customers tended to buy bread in multiples of twenty-five. The very next day, my dad had a carpenter design and build wooden trays to hold twenty-five loaves of bread and he had me pack the first tray.

These were moments I lived for, because I wanted my dad to be proud of me. He was not one to coddle or buoy me up, and I don't recall him ever telling me that he loved me; yet I felt safest when I held his hand. He would wrap his big hand around mine with just the right amount of pressure and I knew that nothing could harm me.

My dad, affectionately known as Mamdu at home and in Ismaili circles, was a well-respected man in the wider community despite never receiving a formal education. He had lawyers from across town seeking his input on contracts and legal disputes. He was a practical joker and nothing made him happier than to laugh and make other people laugh. His laugh was deep and loud and infectious. From him, I learned about work ethic, about giving your all and being passionate about whatever you do, and about being resourceful and finding a way through challenges.

After working with my dad for two years, I left Moshi to come to Canada on vacation. It was December 30, 1978. I did not know then that I would never see him again. He died a few years later in a freak fire accident in the bakery. He was only 52, and I had not seen him in four years. If I had not spent those years working with him, I never would have known his brilliance, learned life lessons from him, or had the vivid memories that I still have about him.

I landed in Toronto and saw snowflakes falling gently from the sky. It felt like a scene straight out of a movie. Everything was a new and thrilling experience—McDonald's and Big Macs, subways that were sleek and fast, doors that opened when you approached, malls the size of small towns, skyscrapers that almost touched the sky, and *Wheel of Fortune* on TV where people made money by solving word puzzles. I found Honest Ed's a fascinating playground, its neon signs inviting you with, "Come in and get lost!" and could easily spend hours going up and down the escalators, delighting in all the sales, and calculating how I was going to spend my few $1 bills to score the best deals.

I fell in love with The Fonz from the sitcom *Happy Days*, and with Toronto hook, line and sinker, and wanted to stay longer. I called my dad to ask him if he would support me financially if I went to school in Canada. I wasn't at all sure what his response would be, but he immediately agreed and I cried with joy. I went to a computer college where I got a diploma in computer programming. Later I enrolled at York University where I graduated with an honors degree in Mass Communication and English.

I met Nagib in the hallowed halls of York University in March 1980. Two weeks after our first meeting, Nagib declared that he would marry me one day. I was quizzical. Friendship blossomed into love. On a cold November 20, 1980, at 3:20 PM, at Founders College, York University, Nagib asked me if we could "go steady." It took me a whole five minutes to say yes. Eighteen months later, Nagib got down on his knee and asked me to marry him. I said yes. We were married on May 1, 1982. I was 23 and Nagib was 21.

Nagib and I are diametric opposites. He likes structure and process; I am a free spirit. He is the smartest person I know; I know how to access information when I need it. I have many friends; I am Nagib's best friend. He is the responsible one in our relationship; I am the fun factor in his life. He lives in the world of rational and logical thinking; I am spontaneous and live in the world of curiosity and possibilities. He is a planner with a vision; I am an implementer who gets things done. He espouses patience and moderation; I am impatient and prone to extremes. Somehow, somewhere, we found our way into each other's hearts in a deep and abiding love that makes us both better and more complete.

Four years later, our son Shayne Aman came into our lives and filled it with unexpected play and joy. Eighteen months later, we welcomed our daughter Sabrina Natasha into our home and our hearts. My mom, Zera, whom we sponsored from Tanzania after my dad's death, and my sister, Naznin, joined our family to create a happy family space, a home.

What binds us as a family is our faith. We are Ismaili Muslims, belonging to the Shia branch of Islam, and followers of the Aga Khan, who is our spiritual leader. Every action we take, the way in which we govern our lives, the choices we make—is in accordance with the values of our faith. The values of generosity, humility, service, social conscience, tolerance, human dignity, intellect and balance between the material and spiritual form the cornerstone of who we are and what we do.

For most of my adult life, prior to the cancer diagnoses, I was a Type A personality—competitive, overachieving, ambitious, impatient. I am a human resources practitioner working in the areas of performance, talent, leadership, coaching, change management, and organizational development. I love what I do and have had the privilege of working for several organizations in the financial, retail, insurance, and pharmaceutical industries over the past thirty years. I was at the height of my career, working alongside the senior leadership of an international pharmaceutical company, when an unexpected and unwelcome visitor knocked at my door.

The First Diagnosis

It was February 3, 2012, when Dr Robert Wu, the young internist at Toronto General Hospital, held both my hands and solemnly uttered those fateful words. To say that we were in shock would be a terrible understatement. This was a bad dream, a terrifying nightmare without end.

For several months, I had experienced fatigue, weight loss, and night sweats. I thought this was due to stress at work or menopause. My family doctor ordered blood tests, which indicated that my hemoglobin was dropping rapidly. She had me go to the emergency ward at North York General Hospital, where I received a blood transfusion. The doctors there suggested I get a colonoscopy to find out the cause of the blood loss. The colonoscopy results came back normal, and yet my symptoms continued. When my hemoglobin dropped further, week after week, I checked myself into emergency at Toronto General Hospital, hoping that one of its world-renowned hematologists would get to the bottom of this. Dr Jean Wang, the hematologist on call, attended to me. It was February 2. She ordered extensive blood tests. And even as we sat in the room, awaiting the results, she ordered yet more tests. Nagib became worried and asked Dr Wang what she was looking for. She said it was too early to tell, but the worst-case scenario was cancer. She recommended that I stay at the hospital overnight for a bone-marrow aspiration. Late that night, Nagib went home to catch some sleep. On the way, he called me from the car, sounding heartbroken. He said the walk to the car had been cold, dark, and dismal, and that reflected his state of mind. He said that a cloud was hanging over us and we needed to be prepared for the worst.

"How long do I have to live?" The words were barely audible behind my tears.

"That's variable," said Dr Wu.

For someone who has lived a healthy, vibrant, exciting life, never been to hospital (except to give birth), rarely even taken a Tylenol, this was unbearable. Nagib and I sat shell-shocked on the hospital bed. How do you deal with such a fateful diagnosis, a death sentence pronounced with such equanimity, when you have so much to offer to the world? So much more to experience and see? So much love to give? So many plans made as a family, as a couple? I thought of my husband, my mom, my son and daughter.

How can you bear to listen to your love and partner of more than thirty years cry in his sleep? How do you deal with your son telling you that he is afraid you are going to die? How do you prepare to share this news with your daughter who is halfway around the world? How do you tell your eighty-two-year-old mom that you have advanced cancer and help her make sense of this news when you are doing the same?

All I could think about in the moment was that I was going to die. My mind raced with an unending stream of questions. Whom should I call and tell about my cancer? Who would preside over my funeral? What arrangements could I make to lessen the stress on my family? Was my will in order? Was I up on my burial insurance? And then the irrational thoughts: had I been a good daughter, partner, and mother? Should I leave letters for my children, begging their forgiveness? A letter for my husband, for all the arguments we had? My emotions were all over the place. I believed that I had six months to live and there was a lot to do.

After the shock wore off a little, I got into planning mode. One of the first things I did, while still in hospital, was to call a contractor and ask him to install hardwood floors at the entrance, in the kitchen, and in the family room of our home. As irrational as this seems, I figured that when I died, grieving guests would gather in the house, and it should be presentable. Looking back, I think I was trying to take some control over my life, because there was so much I had lost control of.

When I returned home from the hospital, I continued to live at a frantic pace because I thought I was on borrowed time. I ordered and installed new curtains for the living room. Nagib and I went out on dates and treasured every minute. Friends and family started dropping by in the evenings and weekends with carrot cakes and flowers. Most of these get-togethers ended with beautiful recitations of prayers. I continued to work every day, except when I had to go for tests at the hospital.

Cancer is probably one of the most dreaded words in the English language, a "monster that cannot be named." We find it difficult to talk about, we have trouble hearing about it, and we are terrified by the thought of it. While I was grappling with myeloma, worse news was waiting in the wings.

Jacques Funeral Home—Nagib's Story

It was the winter of 1979 when I answered the hallway phone in our university residence with, "Jacques Funeral Home, how may I help you?" The girl at the other end of the line was flustered and was about to hang up when I said, "No, no. I'm joking. Who are you looking for?" It was Munira, asking for Karim, a friend of hers from Tanzania who lived in the same residence as me at York University.

Fast forward several months and I was introduced to Munira by another mutual friend at Central Square cafeteria, where we all hung out between classes. "I know that voice," she said, as soon as she heard me speak. "Aren't you Jacques Funeral Home?" And so began our acquaintance.

It was not until a frosty day in November, when my friend Alnashir and I picked up Munira on the way to the university that Munira and I really got close. Rebellious Munira, standing on the sidewalk in sub-zero temperatures—wearing open-toed shoes, no gloves, no hat—jumps into the car, her teeth chattering from the cold. I immediately grabbed her hands and started rubbing them to warm them. And that began our courtship, which culminated in our getting married while still in school.

Like Munira, I too was born in Tanzania to Ismaili Muslim parents of East Indian origin. Unlike Munira, I grew up in Mahuta, a small village in Mtwara region in the south, where we didn't have electricity in the first few years of my life, and running water had only been made available to the Indian shopkeepers of the village the year I was born. From these humble beginnings, my father, with only a primary school education, built a business conglomerate in Mtwara, consisting of a textile factory specializing in men's shirts, a sandals factory, a cashew nut plant and, best of all, a candy factory. He was on his way to expanding into construction in the burgeoning economy of the Tanzanian south, when Julius Nyerere, the first President of Tanzania, implemented Ujamaa, a political concept that espoused socialism. Overnight, my father and many other merchants, mostly Indian, had their businesses and properties seized by the government and were made to work as employees in these same businesses. Fearing for our safety, my parents sent me and my younger sister and brother, accompanied by my grandparents and extended family members, on a boat to Pakistan. Shortly after arriving in Karachi in August 1971, we found ourselves ensnared in the tensions of the India-Pakistan war of 1971, which resulted in the creation of the state of Bangladesh. After the end of the war, I was shipped off to a boarding school in Abbottabad, in the northern areas of Pakistan. By a strange coincidence, Abbottabad is the same military town in which Osama bin Ladin hid until he was killed by United States Navy SEALs in a daring raid in 2010.

In February 1974, my family immigrated to Canada, where I attended junior high school and high school before enrolling at York University, where the "Jacques Funeral Home" incident occurred.

It's difficult being on the other end of bad news. It's even more difficult when the bad news isn't about you but about the person you love most in the world. Friday, February 3, 2012, 4:08 PM, I held Munira's hands tightly as Dr Wu finished his sentence, " . . . multiple myeloma, an incurable cancer of the blood."

My heart started pounding, and I silently began reciting prayers for help. The doctor continued talking and explaining in as kind a manner as he could. I watched the shock and disbelief in Munira's eyes. "Am I going to die?" she asked. "It's variable . . . ," he answered slowly. Further tests would be required to determine how far the cancer had spread and the prognosis for recovery. For tonight, he said, we will give you another blood transfusion and you can go home. Someone will contact you with an appointment with an oncologist.

And then, suddenly, the tables turned. Muni reached for the doctor's hand and said, "I'm so sorry for you, that you have to give me this bad news. Are you okay?" I watched in disbelief, overcome by love and admiration for her.

And that's the way it's been since the diagnosis. Munira deals with it by letting reality sink in, then her compassion steps up, followed by questions—a thirst for learning everything that we need to know to battle this monster. I admire this most about Muni. Her ability to see what is happening to her, to feel it—intensely—yet not be afraid to express it. And then, turning it into a mission.

As for me, I had a sickly feeling in my stomach, like I wanted to throw up as soon as we heard the diagnosis. I had an awful, unshakable realization that our lives going forward would never be the same again. And then, while we were still in the hospital room, with an iPad in hand, we Googled "multiple myeloma" and sorted through all the information and misinformation we found online so that we could properly convey the news to our friends and family.

We are people of faith. To despair is to give up on God. We don't know why these things happen to us. We must accept and, yes, grieve and get angry if we want to, but as one friend emailed us, "The will of God never takes you to where the grace of God will not protect you."

And so began our battle with cancer.

The Diagnosis—Shayne's Story

I remember that day so well. February 3, 2012. Sitting at my desk in downtown Toronto in my light-grey tailored suit and Italian leather shoes. Sipping my second coffee of the day—a short blonde roast from Starbucks with nonfat milk and a Splenda. Working on yet another urgent pitch book for an important client meeting the following week. The typical life of an investment banker.

But today was going to be different. It was Friday and an old friend from university was in town; we had planned to catch up over dinner later that night. It was around 2 PM and my phone buzzed. A text message from my dad: "Mom's blood count is low again. We are at the hospital." I glanced at my phone, took a sip of coffee, and went back to work. I'm sure it's nothing.

A couple of hours passed and another message: "You should come to the hospital." I read the message, but my mind quickly shifted back to the task at hand. I just had to finish the pitch book and send it out, and then maybe I could swing by the hospital on my way to dinner. Plus, my boss *needed* the draft that evening so that he could review it and provide his comments over the weekend. How could I leave work right now?

Another hour passed. I was making good progress but had caught a couple of mistakes in the numbers that I had to correct. Another message: "Shayne, are you coming?" I hastily wrote back: "Can't right now. Will come by later." I was tired, over-caffeinated and unable to think about anything other than finishing work as quickly as possible, so that I could take a well-deserved night off before returning to the office for a weekend full of work.

I was rushing my last edits. It was now 8:30 PM and I was already late for dinner. I had told my friend to grab a taxi and get a table at the restaurant; I'd be there soon. I messaged my dad to find out how everything was at the hospital. "Mom is getting a second blood transfusion. We'll be heading home shortly. You really should have come." I apologized and told him I'd see them in the morning. They're used to this, I figured. Plus, tomorrow is Saturday. I could probably spare a few hours and have breakfast with them at home before heading to the office. I finished the pitch book, emailed it out and rushed over to the restaurant to meet my friend. He was in medical school at the time and when he heard that my mom had received her second blood transfusion in three weeks, he looked concerned. "Does she have any other symptoms? Does she have internal bleeding? What could be causing it?" I quickly changed the subject and we reminisced about the good old days at university, when life seemed much simpler and more exciting. An hour later, my usual driver Khalid was waiting for me outside the restaurant. "Long day? You look tired. Going home or out somewhere?" he asked, with a smile. "Home, please. I need my bed." I slumped over in the backseat and dozed off on the thirty-minute drive home. My parents' lights were off in their bedroom. No need to wake them up and bother them, I thought. I snuck into my bed.

I never told my mom this but the next morning, when she and my dad shared their devastating news at the breakfast table, I was struck with an overwhelming sense of guilt. It wasn't shock or even sadness that brought me to tears—it was guilt. How could I have not gone to the hospital and been by their side when they received the worst news of their lives? That was my job in our family—to be there, to be strong, to tell a joke and lighten the mood in the darkest of times. What could have possibly been so important at work that going to the hospital hadn't even crossed my mind? Why didn't I just cancel dinner with my friend and come home early? When did I become so self-absorbed? Who had I become? I sat in my mom's arms and wept quietly as she talked about how her life, my dad's life, all of our lives would never be the same again.

The Diagnosis—Sabrina's Story 1

Buzz Buzz. That's the sound my phone makes when someone's thinking about me. It's a message, an email, and they come even at odd hours of the night. When you're living in Africa and 7,500 miles away from home, buzz buzz is indeed the best sound in the world. It is the sound of being loved.

The best buzzes are from your parents reminding you that no matter how old you are, or how far you are, you're still very much a part of their lives. I woke up that particular morning to a much different message from my parents—one that said, Let's talk. I quickly did the math and realized it was one o'clock in the morning their time. That's never a good sign.

Dazed and slightly jet-jagged from having flown from Italy the night before, I cuddled up with my computer in the spot that receives the best network connection—an idiosyncrasy you learn when living abroad. Through muffled Skype video chat, I heard three words that have not left my head since: *I have cancer.* My mom—my beautiful fifty-three-year-old mother who has been my inspiration, my coach, my rock, my role model, my best friend. My mom. Cancer.

As soon as I heard those three words, the tears started rolling down. I listened to my mom and dad tell me what they knew so far, but I was too shocked to make sense of any of it. Low hemoglobin. Blood transfusion. Bone marrow test. Cancer.

We decided to end the call after the fifth time the connection cut and promised to talk more the next day. With all my friends in Canada fast asleep or unreachable, I curled up on my couch overwhelmed with sadness. I was sad that my parents had to bear the burden of waiting for a whole week before telling me the news. I can only imagine how tough it was for them to have kept it from me while I was sending "wish you were here" emails from Milan. I was sad that I could not be there for my mom while she was grappling with the biggest news ever given to her. I was sad for all the pain I knew was in store for her, just when she had reached the peak of her life. I also began questioning my decisions in life: why am I so far away from home? Did I make the wrong decision to work abroad when I could have been spending time with my mom?

I'm not sure how many minutes passed before I snapped back to reality and realized I was running late for a flight to Dar es Salaam. I really didn't want to go. In fact, the last thing I wanted to do was put on an everything's-okay-face with my colleagues while my heart and my mind were with my family in Canada. I needed time to sit with a tub of ice cream and just be, just process. But the meetings were with international partners that had been planned months in advance and could not be re-scheduled. I quickly dumped the Italy jackets and boots out of my suitcase and stuffed in summer dresses for Tanzania. I hopped into a taxi, checked in at the airport, tears sporadically coming through against my best effort to be strong. I told the first person I met in Dar es Salaam that my mom had just been diagnosed with blood cancer, the news bubbling and bursting out of me, unable to stay inside any longer. "It's all the microwaves and technology you people use in the West," he said candidly. "Really?" I thought in my head. "My mom may be dying and that's the first thing you say?" I nodded and decided not to mention the news to anyone else that trip, uncertain if their response would bring me to tears or make me want to bop them across the head. When I returned to Nairobi, my boss graciously accepted my decision to finish my contract from Toronto so that I could be closer to my mom. I booked a one-way ticket to Toronto and flew out on February 26, 2012, closing the eighteen-month Kenya chapter of my life. It was now time to gear up for another chapter—probably, the most challenging but life-changing one our family would ever have to go through. *Kwaheri* Kenya, *Karibu* Canada.

But It Was Not Just One Cancer

The week following my diagnosis of myeloma, I was back at work, sitting at my desk, preparing to facilitate an executive leadership meeting. The phone rang. I picked it up and heard an unfamiliar voice. "Mrs Premji?" It was the hematologist at Toronto General Hospital, Dr Wang. Strange, I thought, I'm not expecting any calls from the hospital. "We've had a chance to look at the results from your bone marrow biopsy and we'd like you to come in for more tests," she said. "Can you come today?" I could hear the gravity in her voice. "Is everything OK?" I managed to ask. She said something to the effect that my bone marrow was showing unusual activity. I told her that I would be at the hospital the following day. Somehow, I managed to run a great meeting, and then rushed back to my office to be alone. I shut the door, closed my eyes, took a breath, and called Nagib with the news. Nagib tried to comfort me, but we were still raw from the news of the earlier diagnosis of myeloma and had very little left to give each other. What could be worse, we thought, than the news we were already dealing with? We soon found out.

Further bone marrow tests revealed a second cancer, lymphoma, in my body. Dr Wang referred me to Dr Rodger Tiedemann, an oncologist at Princess Margaret Hospital (as it was called then), who had experience with both lymphoma and multiple myeloma. Before we met Dr Tiedemann, my son Shayne had begun researching doctors and facilities in Canada and the US that we needed to consider for a second opinion. Shayne approached this task with rigor, using Excel sheets and all. Nagib and Shayne were both with me for my first appointment with Dr Tiedemann on February 22, 2012.

We waited in one of his clinic rooms, taking turns standing or sitting on one of the two chairs provided, until a tall, blue-eyed doctor with boyish good looks entered. "I'm Rodger," he said, shaking hands with each of us. Wearing a blue oxford shirt with the top button opened, he spoke in a distinctive New Zealand accent. "Wow, he's young," I thought silently. I could see that the same thought had crossed Nagib's mind. But it took only a matter of minutes for him to win us over. He was compassionate and listened with concern and empathy to our fears and worries. He spared time for questions and discussions. He explained to us complex research in a way in which we could understand. I was immensely impressed by his manner, by his knowledge. Though soft-spoken, he was confident. I was convinced that he was uniquely qualified to deal with both myeloma and lymphoma. He performed a physical exam of my lymph nodes and did a bone marrow biopsy in the clinic. He then ordered a series of blood tests and all possible kinds of imaging—X-rays, CT, MRI, and PET scans.

Dr Tiedemann balanced head with heart, and knowledge with humility. In his office you felt seen and you felt heard. And his ability to recall and retain information without taking notes was remarkable. After our meeting, Nagib, Shayne, and I sat down for lunch and reviewed the entire session for two hours. What did we think of Dr T? How were we all feeling? Did we have any concerns? The verdict was unanimous. Dr Tiedemann was the right doctor for me, and in that moment, we put our faith in him with no intention of seeking another opinion. Shayne put away his carefully crafted Excel spreadsheet.

On March 8, 2012, two weeks after our first meeting, Nagib, Shayne, Sabrina (who had just returned from Nairobi), and I went to see Dr Tiedemann for a scheduled follow-up appointment, where he confirmed the diagnoses of Diffuse large B-cell lymphoma, a very aggressive type of non-Hodgkin lymphoma, which had advanced to Stage 4 (the highest stage), coupled with IgG kappa multiple myeloma, which had advanced to Stage 3 and was treatable, but not curable. I heard him mouth the words but could not fathom the message. All I remember is holding on to the chair so tightly that I could feel my veins throbbing.

Dr Tiedemann recommended that we treat the non-Hodgkin lymphoma immediately and put the multiple myeloma on hold. He was very clear. If we did not get the lymphoma under control, I would not make it. The gravity in his tone was unmistakable

Because lymphoma cells move through the body, surgery is not a treatment option. Chemotherapy and / or radiation are generally used. My treatment for lymphoma would consist of six full-day chemotherapy treatments called R-CHOP that would take place every three weeks for about four months, starting the next day, March 9. I was preparing myself mentally to begin the treatment process, but first I had to wait for the results of that morning's blood tests. Little did I know that the worst was yet to come.

The Day Before My First Chemo

The day before my first chemo session, I was at Dr Tiedemann's clinic at Princess Margaret Hospital to get clearance to start treatment. I remember feeling tired when we got to the clinic and I put that down to nerves and a restless night. After a routine blood test, he was shocked to see that my hemoglobin count had plummeted to 42 (the normal value for women is 120-160), from 90 the week before. The previously calm Dr Tiedemann appeared a bit flustered. He kept asking me how I was feeling, apparently surprised that I was standing so calmly before him. He kept looking at the numbers and then back at me. At one time, he actually wondered if there might have been an error in the blood work. I told him I was fine and started to describe the boisterous karaoke party we had hosted the night before with friends. But he was having none of it and said that I needed to go to an emergency department immediately. I thought he was overreacting, but quickly acquiesced when I saw how serious he looked. Princess Margaret, being a specialized cancer-care facility, did not have an Emergency Department. The closest was right across the street at the Toronto General Hospital. I suggested that I could walk over to Emergency—a three-minute walk—and he said that he had already called for an ambulance to take me there. One arrived, and Sabrina and I got into it, while Nagib and Shayne walked over to Toronto General Hospital. When Sabrina and I arrived at the hospital, Nagib and Shayne were waiting for us and we waved at them sheepishly. I even asked Nagib to take a picture of me while I was in the ambulance, so that I could use it for my blog, which I had just started. I realized that the situation was serious when I got to the emergency room and my case was made a priority. The ER staff kept looking at the paperwork wondering how a person with a hemoglobin count of 42 could look so well, speak in coherent sentences, and happily chatter away with her family.

Shortly after I was seen by an emergency doctor, I was lying on a bed in a curtained-off room when I overheard a phone conversation that the doctor was having outside about the patient in Bed 9, beside me. Apparently, the woman was in critical condition and her organs would begin shutting down if they did not begin a blood transfusion immediately. It appeared that the person on the other end of the line was not in favor of this decision. They began a heated discussion until the doctor exclaimed "She is my patient and I'm making the call to start the blood transfusion immediately! If we don't start it now, she *will* die!" Our sympathies reached out to this woman. Who could she be, where was her family? We became quiet. And then in that moment we overheard the doctor correct himself, "Oh sorry, not Bed 9, it's Bed 8."

I was in Bed 8.

The thought hit me, I am going to die today, at Toronto General Hospital, here in Bed 8. I had never thought this way before, that I was on the verge of death. I will never forget the feeling I had as Nagib, Shayne, and Sabrina stood around my bed and together we recited our evening prayers. I looked at each of them, registering their faces, and thought that this was the last time we would pray together. The doctors had said that there was a fifty percent chance that I would not make it through the night. My hemoglobin level had now dropped to a dangerously low 36, and the doctors warned us that my organs would start shutting down one by one. I needed a very specific blood type, since my body had created antibodies that would kill me if I was transfused with the wrong type. The problem was that it would take at least six hours for the hospital to make sure that I received the right type of blood. I did not have six hours. Nagib and I contemplated getting our mukhi, the main religious minister at the jamatkhana we attended, to administer last rites. We began arranging to get my mom and sister to the hospital so they could see me for the last time.

At 8 PM, the doctors rushed me from emergency to intensive care. I asked them what the plan was and they said they would transfuse me with four units of blood that had been partially cross-checked against mine. The first few minutes of each transfusion would be critical; my body would either accept it or reject it. I asked them what Plan B was if my body rejected a unit. They seemed somewhat puzzled that I did not understand the magnitude of the situation. There was no Plan B.

I was scared. My heart was racing. I started to think about the last words I would say to Nagib, Shayne, and Sabrina. What could I tell them that they could hold on to for the rest of their lives? I could not think of anything. I turned to God and asked Him to give me more time on earth. I bargained with God. I promised that I would help people and serve his vision. I promised to be more tolerant and patient. I promised to live my life in a way that would make Him proud. I made a lot of promises that night.

God answered in the form of the hematologist Dr Christine Cserti and her team. They worked diligently, late into the night, to find the blood match in record time. If they had not done that, my end would have come that night at the hospital. The very next day, much to everyone's surprise, I walked out of the intensive care unit and was admitted into the general ward.

I was pleasantly surprised when Dr Cserti came to see me in the general ward the next day. She marveled at the fact that I was up and about and on my iPad, writing. She sat down with me for half an hour to diagram on a sheet of paper the war that had taken place in my body between the good and the bad blood cells, and how miraculous it was that I had survived. The significance of her words choked me up. I knew that God had a hand in keeping me alive. The question I asked myself was, "For what purpose?"

The Diagnosis—Sabrina's Story 2

On March 8, my dad, my brother Shayne, and I sat huddled around my mom's hospital bed in the emergency room, reciting our evening prayer together. The mood was somber and quiet—a change from our normal Premji positivity—interrupted only by an occasional moan of anguish from one of us. The doctors had said there was a fifty percent chance that my mom would not make it through the night. And for the first time since hearing about the cancer diagnosis, I realized that this might be the day I would lose her.

Rewind seven hours.

We arrived at Princess Margaret Hospital for an appointment with my mom's oncologist Dr Tiedemann and a pre-chemotherapy class. Because my mom had been feeling weak the past few days, Dr Tiedemann insisted that she get her blood levels checked prior to starting chemotherapy the next morning. The blood levels showed a critically low hemoglobin count of 42. In that moment, cancer took a backseat and the focus became her blood.

To put this into context, the average woman on the street operates at a hemoglobin level of 120-160, and anything under 50 is considered life-threatening. Given the urgency of the situation, Mom was taken by ambulance across the street to Toronto General Hospital. Upon preparation for a blood transfusion, test results showed that her red blood cells were "bursting," due to what was believed to be an army of antibodies she had built up in response to the initial two transfusions she had received in January and February, when they were still trying to figure out what was wrong with her. Her normal red blood cells were getting killed in the crossfire, a condition known as acute hyper hemolytic anemia.

Mom's an antibody-maker—her body makes antibodies to fight off any foreign substance that comes in contact with her. That's probably why she has never been significantly sick before, but these antibodies were proving to be detrimental to her present condition.

She needed blood and needed it fast; yet, an imperfect blood match would have caused her immune system to attack the new blood cells, turning her own red blood cells into innocent casualties of this war. But if we waited the six to eight hours needed to find a perfect blood match, Mom's hemoglobin could drop even further, putting her at a significant risk of organ failure. We were balancing between the needs of the emergency medicine department to transfuse blood immediately and the hematology specialists to transfuse the right blood. By 8 PM her hemoglobin count had dropped to 36. They rushed her to the intensive care unit—pale-faced, with an oxygen mask and machines beeping.

Just as we were beginning to lose hope, we received word that four units of semi-matched blood had been found. A miracle beyond measure. While our faith was being tested, a team of hematologists led by Dr Christine Cserti was working hard in the blood bank to find the perfect blood match. It's almost like while we were questioning God's plans, God was busy in the blood bank saying, "Guys, it's okay, I got this."

The four bags of blood were our last hope—we asked the intensive care doctors what the plan was if the blood didn't work and were told "steroids, until we figure out what to do." With a risky Plan A and no Plan B, we focused our energy on befriending the blood, giving them the names of Mr Bean, Dexter, Edward Cullen and Popat.

We sat beside her, hearts racing, tears rolling down our cheeks, prayers on our lips, and watched those first drops of blood make their way into her body. Drip, drip, drip. If her body was going to reject the blood, we would know within the first few minutes. A nurse was by her side monitoring every vital sign. I have never been more scared. And we have never prayed harder. I am not entirely certain whether it was the steroids or a dose of romance in Mr Bean's blood, but as the new blood seeped through her veins, Mom slipped her oxygen mask to the side and began to serenade my dad with the love song, "Perhaps, perhaps, perhaps." I didn't know whether to force her to put her mask on properly so she could get every ounce of air her lungs needed, or to simply appreciate that in the last moments of her life, my mom had found a way to infuse fun into our lives. I squeezed her hand harder and looked away, not wanting her to see me cry.

Four hours later, Mr Bean had gone through successfully—but we were not out of the woods yet. Since the four units came from four different people, it was possible that Mom's body would reject any one of the remaining three bags. We watched Dexter, then Edward Cullen, go through. Next blood reading: 51. Great sign. It was the Popat power of the last bag of blood that pushed her hemoglobin up and over a safe threshold—it had reached 91 at 1 PM on Friday afternoon. (And so it came to be that Shayne's first-born child would have the name Popat.)

Mom was moved from ICU into the general ward the following day and was released on Sunday afternoon when it was determined that her hemoglobin levels had remained stable.

Thursday, March 8, 2012 was the scariest day of my life. But it was also a day when I felt more grateful than I have ever been. Miracle #1—Mom could have collapsed at any point that week and would have been rushed to our closest hospital, North York General, and infused with unmatched blood. Given her status as an "antibody-maker," her body would have rejected the blood and she would not have survived. But instead, her low hemoglobin was caught by a routine pre-chemotherapy blood test and acute hyper hemolytic anemia was detected before it was too late to do something about it.

Miracle #2—When the test results came back earlier that day, confirming an aggressive, late-stage lymphoma, the oncologist wrote up a prescription to start chemotherapy the following day. But by the time the nurse called the chemo day care unit, it was five minutes after it had closed, and instead Mom was scheduled for the first chemo session the following Monday. If Mom had started chemo with a hemoglobin of 42 (because a week prior it had been 90 and she had been cleared for chemo), her body would not have been strong enough to take the toxic drugs and she would not have survived.

Miracle #3—Four different blood donors with the exact antibodies to combat Mom's Y and C antibodies were found within thirty minutes. Generally, this takes six to eight hours, since the blood bank has to screen for twenty different variables. We owe our gratitude to Dr Cserti and her team for working nonstop until they found the right blood.

That night, I had almost lost hope. But it was in those moments of despair that I witnessed firsthand the power of prayer, the power of holding on, the power of giving it everything you've got. I have a renewed sense of faith that some force pretty powerful is on my mom's side and therefore these cancers stand absolutely no chance against her strength and courage.

She will survive.

2.

LYMPHOMA

Lymphoma at a Glance

What Is Non-Hodgkin Lymphoma?

Non-Hodgkin lymphoma is a cancer that starts in the lymphocytes of the lymphatic system. The lymphatic system is a system of vessels and organs that run throughout the body. It is part of the body's immune system that fights infections and helps fluids move through the body. Non-Hodgkin lymphoma occurs when the lymphocytes multiply uncontrollably.

Non-Hodgkin lymphoma can start anywhere in the body, for instance, in the neck, armpits or in the groin, and can spread to any tissue or organ through the lymphatic system or the bloodstream. There are more than 60 different types of non-Hodgkin lymphoma.

Non-Hodgkin Lymphoma Statistics

In 2019, an estimated 10,000 Canadians will be diagnosed with non-Hodgkin lymphoma and 2,700 Canadians will die from it. The five-year survival rate for non-Hodgkin lymphoma is 68%. (The ten-year survival rate is 59%.)

Symptoms

Lymphoma can be tough to diagnose because the symptoms are similar to those of flu or a viral infection. In addition to swollen lymph nodes, other signs are fever, night sweats, lack of energy, loss of appetite, and unexplained weight loss.

Treatment

Because lymphoma cells move through the body, surgery is not an option for treatment. Chemotherapy and / or radiation are most commonly used. There are several tests to diagnose lymphoma, including a physical exam of the lymph nodes, imaging tests (X-rays), computer tomography (CT) scans, magnetic resonance imaging (MRI), positron emission tomography (PET) scans, blood tests, and bone marrow tests.

Source:

https://www.cancer.ca

The Darnedest Things People Tell You When You Have Cancer

The news of my cancer has been met with a dizzying array of reactions. Some people have showered me with love, offered heartfelt prayers, and filled my house with flowers, carrot cake, and Cadbury Whole Nut chocolates from England. Others have come with motivational plaques, books telling me what to eat, and comments that confound, confuse, and just make me laugh. Here is my top ten list of the darnedest things people tell you when you have cancer:

10) "My [mother / neighbor / colleague / wife's second cousin twice removed] also had cancer . . . and died."

Believe it or not, this is usually the first thing that comes out of people's mouths! To this day I still don't know how to respond. Shayne suggested that I reply with: "Sorry for your loss. Did they leave you anything in their will?"

9) "How could this happen to someone as nice as you and who has done so much for the community?"

"I guess I didn't do enough?" "Maybe if I had just been ten percent nicer, cancer wouldn't have chosen me?" In reality, this comment makes me want to scream. Cancer does not discriminate. It chooses all kinds of people, good and bad, young and old, fitness enthusiasts and couch potatoes.

8) "This is just a test" or "God is testing you."

This is usually said in a very philosophical tone and I'm almost scared to ask what the person means. I like to respond to this deeply serious comment with some humor: "I hope it's not multiple choice; I've always been bad at those!"

7) "Look at the bright side . . . now you finally have time to take off work and concentrate on yourself."

When people tell me this, I almost want to reply sarcastically: "You know, I never even thought about that. I am so happy to have a good excuse to finally focus on myself!" Only years later will I realize that they may have been onto something.

6) "You should really try eating more [vitamins / turmeric / apple cider vinegar / goji berries etc.] or look into [cannabis oil / radiation-eating black fungus / etc.]!"

Comments like these are usually prefaced by "I was watching this documentary" or "I was reading this email chain forwarded by a friend"; sometimes they even end with the person lowering their voice, looking around warily and whispering " . . . but Big Pharma doesn't want you to know about it." I just smile and thank them for their suggestion.

5) "You look great for someone who has cancer."

Cancer does some interesting things to the body. I have noticed how sometimes my face is puffy because of high doses of prednisone; sometimes it is sallow and painfully thin because I'm eating so little. Wrinkles have appeared where there were none. It takes effort to look and feel good when your body is fighting so hard. I know it comes from a good place, but the last thing you want is for someone to make you more self-conscious about how you look, particularly when you are already your own biggest critic and the mirror is showing you the subtle (and not-so-subtle) changes that come from the ravages of cancer. Except when I fool people into thinking my wigs are my real hair. "I love your hair like this / Did you get your hair done / Wow, who is your hairdresser?" That, I don't mind!

x

4) "You have to account for whatever you did in your past life . . . (sometimes followed by) you have no choice."

Another deeply philosophical comment that usually comes from an individual who is gazing into the distance with a pensive look on their face. I really don't know what to make of this one. Is the person implying that I did something gravely wrong in my past life and that this is my karma? I have enough trouble keeping track of what I have done in this life, let alone what I may have done in a past life. The next time I hear this statement I think I will reply with: "Yes, I am almost positive that in a past life I was a New York Yankees fan and this is payback for supporting the Evil Empire."

3) "You may as well enjoy your life now . . . "

Why? Because I don't have much time to live? It makes me think, "But I have lived fully! Before cancer, I squeezed every moment out of every day. Now that I have cancer, I don't plan on stopping all of a sudden." I then resolve that I will prove the naysayers wrong and live a long, healthy, and productive life.

2) "How long did the doctors give you?"

I find it so interesting that some people can actually come out and ask a question like that. But it has happened to me more than once, most recently by a taxi driver who was driving me to the hospital. Maybe he was trying to determine if I would stick around long enough to be a regular customer! This question can be quite depressing, and so lately I've decided to flip the script: "They said it's really up to me. I'm thinking maybe another thirty or forty years? Definitely long enough to see the Blue Jays win another World Series. Yeah, so probably at least forty years. How about you? How long do you have?"

1) You should practice positivity. Being positive is more effective than [chemo / radiation / surgery / seeing your doctor].

The underlying message is that positivity can cure cancer. And no matter how lousy you are feeling, how much pain you're in, how scared you are, you must not express it, because, God forbid, any negative emotion can cause the cancer to multiply out of control. I just nod my head, knowing that they mean well.

What I have cherished are interactions with people who take that first step, however uncomfortable, to acknowledge that I have cancer. Acknowledgment without minimizing the situation or overreacting, without trying to fix it or look for a silver lining; without reminding me to be strong and positive. It sounds something like this: "I'm really sorry for what you are going through. It sucks. I want you to know that I am thinking of you and keeping you in my prayers. What can I do to support you?" This creates the space for sadness, for tears, and perhaps even a conversation.

A Carefully Concocted Cocktail of Drugs

March 12, 2012

Today I start chemotherapy.

I am extremely nervous because I don't know what to expect. My mind is swirling with images from movies about cancer patients who look haggard and are confined to their beds and need help to breathe. Articles about the side effects of chemo have heightened my anxiety. I am afraid of what chemo will do to me. I am afraid that I won't be able to work while I'm in treatment. I am afraid that my body will not tolerate the drugs—and then what?

The chemo experience is systematic and organized. You check in at chemo day care at the appointed time, and the attendant at the reception desk gives you a buzzer that will vibrate when it is your time for treatment. It is as if you are waiting for your table to be called at a restaurant: "Premji, party of four!" Then you wait, and wait. And wait some more, sometimes for two hours. When your medication is ready, the receptionist sends you to one of the colorful pods and a designated seat (Purple Pod, Chair 12 in my case). Cheerful volunteers with big smiles come over to offer apple and cranberry juices, lend a helping hand, and stay to chat if you want. Slowly they will become part of your new family, the familiar faces in a maze of sterile hallways.

To my surprise, the actual chemo experience is less daunting than I expected. You sit in a comfortable leather chair, talk to family, have lunch, take a nap. All the while, drugs enter your body drip by drip. I expected to get sick immediately after chemo, but that wasn't the case. Instead, I went to Willowdale Jamatkhana that evening to say a prayer of gratitude.

Each chemo treatment, as I will come to learn, adds to the effect of the previous one—and it requires longer and longer for the healthy cells to rebuild. Chemo targets and kills the rapidly dividing cancer cells in the body. But there are normal cells in the body that are also rapidly dividing, such as hair follicles, and chemo attacks these good cells as well, with a negative effect on the body. Each dose of chemo kills only a small percentage of cancer cells. Therefore, multiple treatments are required to destroy as many cancer cells as possible. The negative effects of chemo then add up and get worse. Hair loss is one of them.

To help me cope, I visualize the chemo as a light, warming and filling my body, helping me attack the cancer cells inside me. I imagine the cancer cells pouring out of my body. I pray that the chemo does its work quickly so I can return to a normal life.

The Magical Hat—Sabrina

There are two types of people in this world—those who can wear hats, and those who can't. Unfortunately, my mom was always the latter type. For years, we had tried to find a hat that liked her—from baseball caps at Blue Jays baseball games to visors on beach vacations, and from Santa hats at Christmas parties, to beanies, berets, and bowlers. If it's been invented, we have tried it.

On Monday, while waiting for our first chemotherapy experience at the Princess Margaret Hospital, a hat found its way to my mom. Not just any hat—*the* hat. A bright pink-and-white, handmade toque that was a perfect fit. Like Cinderella's glass slipper. Mom had found a hat that agreed with her, and the hat had found a new home.

But this particular hat was more than just a hat; it was an act of kindness. It was made by a past cancer survivor who wanted to pay forward the generosity given to her during her experience with cancer. In today's society, kindness has often taken a backseat to greed, and generosity has been demoted to something we *can* do, rather than something we *should* do. The giving of time to a worthy cause is a calculated act that must be booked in our calendars weeks in advance.

Never have I been more attuned to our society's values and how they seem to stray ever further from our core human instincts. And then a hat comes our way—and flowers, phone calls, emails, and chocolates from strangers and friends alike. These simple acts of kindness propel my mom towards a place of positivity and promise. A place where she feels she has an army of supporters to get her through this journey. A place where she feels she has something worth fighting for. More and more that reason seems to be to give back, to be able to "pay forward in her turn" all the support that she has received during this time.

The hat has been a reminder of the fragility of life—the idea that we can be at the peak of our careers one day, and the next be bed-ridden in hospital. It is a reminder that life is short, and our moments are too precious to be living a life we do not particularly want. Engaging in habits we don't want. Doing things we are not absolutely passionate about. But most of all, the hat has been a symbol of hope—a silent gift from a complete stranger telling us that everything will be okay.

If the hat-maker could survive cancer, my mom can too. And going through an experience like this, you hang on to every ounce of hope you can get. Every stable hemoglobin level, every normal temperature, every bit of energy is something to be hopeful about and to celebrate.

The hat will become an essential accessory item when my mom begins to lose her hair in the coming weeks. But it has played an even greater role already—to remind us to live each day in gratitude, to be kind to others, to embrace the fragility of life and to remain hopeful.

I Am More Than My Hair . . .

On Sunday, I sensed, rather than felt, my hair separating from my scalp. I was in bed and stayed very still, hoping that if I didn't move, my hair would remain intact. Finally I got up and found the courage to look at myself in the mirror. Relief! My hair was on top of head. Everything was fine with the world. And then I took a shower and observed in painful shock as my hair left my head and collected by my feet.

Hair loss is one of the telltale signs of cancer treatment. It was not a surprise to lose my hair, but why on that day? We were celebrating Sabrina's birthday at home and I was meeting her boyfriend's parents for the first time. I knew how important this day was for her, and I wanted to make a good impression. Couldn't my hair have chosen to fall out the next day?

The doorbell rang, but I was too afraid to go downstairs. How could I, looking like a freak? I needed to be a good host, a good mom, but I was overwhelmed by the avalanche of self-doubt and the need to hide away from the world. I curled up under the covers and shut down. I woke up to Sabrina's anxious face asking me if everything was okay. This was her day, not mine. I composed myself, grabbed her hand and said, "Let's do this."

Hair hurts as it's falling out. And when it started coming out in clumps a few days later, and there was less hair on my head than at my feet, I realized that the time had come for extreme measures.

I called my friend and hairstylist Afsan. We set up time to shave my hair at home on Tuesday night at 8 PM. This had to be planned so that Shayne could be home for the event, at his request. The actual shave happened quite seamlessly. My family cheered on and offered encouraging words. My mom cried. I refused to look in the mirror. Afsan was compassionate, professional, and sensitive. As soon as she left, I wore a colorful scarf to hide my shaved head. That made me feel safe. That was my plan—to scarf my way through the days until my hair grew back. We celebrated by having cheesecake and coffee.

Shaving your head is one thing. Accepting how you look with a shaved head is an entirely different thing. The first morning after the shave, I went to the bathroom and looked at myself in the mirror. I screamed, because I did not recognize myself. Somehow, I had to align what I saw in the mirror with my idea of what I looked like. This was easier said than done. My plan was to stand in front of the mirror for as long as it took and have an honest chat with the reflection I saw. I was going to say, "I am you, and you are me, so let's deal with it." One way or another, I needed to find a way to be comfortable with this new look and embrace it. Besides I didn't want to be scaring myself every morning.

Even when you begin to accept the way you look, that doesn't guarantee that others will. We went to Niagara Falls for a mini vacation. I decided that I would bravely come out in public with my bald head with the encouragement of my family. As soon as I stepped out of the hotel lobby, a young boy started pointing at me and saying something in French to his mom. She was trying to get him to stop staring at me, but the boy persisted. I don't know what he was saying, all I know is that I was an emotional mess. I knew that I looked awkward, with my face all puffy and flushed with medication. I rushed back to the hotel room, shut the door and cried. I put a scarf on and then got back to my anxiously waiting family who, thankfully, did not say anything. Sabrina held my hand tightly, protectively. On that trip, Shayne bought me two berets, a red and a black one. It seemed like a symbolic gesture that life goes on. I have experienced this scenario a few times at the grocery store, at a restaurant, and at a shopping mall, and always with children, who, God bless them, call it as they see it.

Today I pay tribute to my incredible husband. Every time I hide behind a scarf, he gently removes it and tells me I am beautiful bald. He is doing this so often that I am starting to believe him. Sort of.

Memories—Sabrina

March 28, 2012

Last night, my mom snuck into my bed at midnight to wish me happy birthday. Yesterday I turned twenty-four. As she held me in her arms, she told me how she was proud of the person I had become. It has only been a few years since we would lie curled up beside each other in that very bed, talking about first kisses and bad dates, about goals and aspirations, about upcoming tests and interesting things I had learned in school that day, about which university I should go to. Ten years of stories, laughs, tears, and instructions have been shared in this bed.

We thought of the memories we would create together over the next ten years. I imagine my mom being there to drop me off at the airport when I return to East Africa once she gets better—she is a strong woman, but cries every time she hugs me at the security gate. Every time. I imagine calling my mom from abroad, telling her about all the inspiring *mamas* I met in the field that day, and asking her to help me process the inequities and challenges of working in the development sector. I can imagine us figuring out which school I should go to for my master's degree over a plate of nachos and chicken wings. I imagine her being there to decorate the Christmas tree with me when I return home for the holidays each year. Ever since I was a little girl, my mom has told me that the biggest decision I will ever make is deciding who I want to marry. On my wedding day, I imagine her being present every step of the way. To make sure I made the right decision. To dance with my dad at the reception. To continue to show me how love grows stronger even after thirty years of marriage. I imagine my mom holding my hand in the delivery room as I become a mother—and introducing her grandchildren to the enchanting words of Roald Dahl and the magic of Harry Potter.

We are a family of immense faith and positivity, but we are also a family of honest communication. As we visualized the memories we would create over the next decade, we also talked about our fears. For a moment, the thought crossed our minds that maybe my mom would not be there for convocations, Christmases, and carriages. She was battling advanced stages of two types of blood cancer, and there were a number of things that had to align perfectly for her to get through that. Stable blood levels. No more antibodies building during transfusions. Chemotherapy for the lymphoma. Chemotherapy for the multiple myeloma. A stem-cell transplant or two. And hopefully, sometime soon, a cure for myeloma, so she can live well beyond the five to six years typical of people with this type of cancer.

And then we realized that the beauty of life lies in its unpredictability and its changes. I don't know what the next ten years have in store for my mom, or for any of us. But what I do know is that when my mom and I get lost as we generally do, we always seem to stumble across a Fairweather outlet store. And when a new Twilight movie comes out, we are at the front of the line on opening day. And when the Canadian National Exhibition opens each year, we are the happiest people in the world. These are what memories are made of. It's not necessarily the amount of time you have with someone that matters, it's what you make of that time. It's about being present in every conversation, in every moment. That's what really counts.

Everything You Want to Know About Wigs, but Were Afraid to Ask

April 2, 2012

It is time to explore wigs. A wig is a curious thing. I have learned that there is real art in selecting and wearing a wig. And when you do it right, it is a sight to behold.

Wigs come with both real and synthetic hair and there are many options—long hair, short hair, extensions, curly hair, straight hair, blonde hair, and purple hair. And the price range for wigs is all over the place. There are some places where you can get donated wigs for free, and I spoke to someone today who paid $700 for her wig and then added extensions to it, so the total cost was over a thousand dollars.

I enlisted the help of my hairdresser Afsan and my daughter Sabrina to find the perfect wig. They were people on a mission, walking up and down the aisles, bringing first one wig, then another for me to consider. The store had a silly policy of letting you try on no more than four wigs, but when they saw we meant business, they waived the rule. I ended up buying three. One that looks like my own hair, complete with a bit of gray; one that is a bit funkier and has a mind of its own (I'm not sure that I like its mind, so we are still learning to coexist); and a blonde wig that makes me look like JLo. Total cost for all three wigs: less than $200. Cancer has not taken away my ability to bargain.

Buying a wig is one thing. Wearing it correctly is a different story. Over to Afsan, to get the technique right. There are three points you have to focus on: the center of your forehead, and the two points above your temples. If you get these points right, you know that your wig is exactly where it should be. Slightly off and it doesn't quite work. Then you need to ensure that your wig is secure at the back too—there are clips to help you do this.

It takes practice to wear a wig right and it takes time to get used to being comfortable wearing a foreign object on your head. Wigs can be itchy and heavy. They can feel sweaty, particularly in the summer. The upside is that they allow me to play and explore different looks that make me feel sexy and confident.

Even when you've found the perfect wig and secured it properly to your head, mishaps can still happen. There are times, after a social event, when I have hugged many people and my wig just holds on to dear life, lopsided, barely stable.

Last week, I went to Old Navy to buy some clothes. I was having a wonderful time trying on jeans and sweaters, hoodies and tops. There was a young attendant who was helping me with sizes and suggestions. We had perfected a routine where I would try on an outfit and come out of the dressing room. She would look at me and give me the thumbs up or thumbs down depending on how it looked on me.

After about the eighth change, when I emerged out of the dressing room, she screeched. I asked her if she was all right. She hung on to a clothes rack and pointed at me in shock. I went in the dressing room, looked in the mirror and realized that my wig had fallen off my head and was caught on my shoulder. It was quite the sight, my nearly bald head having made an unwelcome appearance. Within minutes, I had gone from being an elegant woman to someone who'd just come from Mars.

The humor of the situation struck me and I started to howl with laughter. In between bursts of laughter, I explained to the attendant that I had cancer. She did not quite know how to react to this news at first but soon she started to laugh too. Next thing I know all the people in the dressing room joined in and we became allies in the moment. It was therapeutic and uplifting.

Since that time, I have added to my wig collection handsomely and now have 13 wigs! I am also learning to rock the bald look. I experiment with berets and scarves. Each look allows me to morph into someone different, without changing the essence of who I am. And it keeps things interesting for Nagib, who is never sure what he is going to encounter when he comes home from work.

Losses, Endings, and New Beginnings

April 6, 2012

Before being diagnosed with cancer, I rarely thought about death. I knew on a rational level that one day we all die, but this was a faraway notion that was not on my radar. There is nothing like cancer to force you to get eyeball to eyeball with the cold grip of mortality; even if the time lines are uncertain.

Today is not a good day for me. I am beginning to see myself as nothing more than a perishable mass with a limited shelf life costing the system thousands of dollars. Yes, I am Munira, I am me, but who am I, what have I become?

Dealing with cancer is not just about managing the physical aspects of the disease; it is equally about figuring out who you are through the process. It comes down to identity. Prior to the cancers, I was very clear about who I was, what was important to me, my beliefs, my values, how I showed up in the world. Now my identity is threatened and I am sitting in this uncomfortable space, wondering how to operate. I feel like I am losing myself.

I feel a loss of purpose in not being able to work. I love my work as a human resources practitioner, and normally I would jump out of bed to start the day with enthusiasm and energy. I didn't realize how difficult it would be not to have a place to go to every morning for eight or nine hours. That is probably the hardest loss for me. Is it a temporary loss? I don't know.

More and more I see myself as a cancer patient, a number, a victim. It's easy to feel this way when you are no longer able to do the things you normally do easily. Chemotherapy is tough on my system and I have become physically dependent. I need help to walk. I need help to climb stairs. I need help to take a bath. It is quite debilitating. I can't remember things like names, or where I left my keys. Mentally I am exhausted. Yesterday, I called somebody, and when they picked up the phone, I could not remember who it was that I was calling. What's happening to me?

There is a part of me that is fueled with the urgency of wanting to do everything now, because at some point it may be too late. One day I started writing letters to my family with instructions to open them after my death, but the neuropathy in my fingers made it impossible to write more than a few sentences. When I am on steroids, I am as high as a kite, rushing here and there, interested in everything, taking on more than I can handle. I wear my family down with my mania, and then, finally, when the effects of the steroids wear off, I crash and sleep and cry a lot.

I've lost my financial independence. I worked as an independent consultant and relied on contract work to earn a living. Now suddenly I am not earning and must go on disability assistance. This has been a shock to my system and my pride has taken a hit. Pre-cancer, I would identify five charities that I would support each year because giving to vulnerable people was part of what I did. Now I am one of the vulnerable ones. I think long and hard before I buy another dress or book. I have started shopping at the dollar stores for household items. When friends call me about lunch, I make excuses because I can no longer afford lunch dates, and offer to meet them for a coffee instead. I am making choices of economy like taking the 401 rather than the 407 toll road for trips; or taking the bus and subway to get to Princess Margaret Hospital, rather than driving and paying $25 for parking; or purchasing books on my Kindle rather than the more expensive physical copies; or having the cleaning lady come every couple of months, rather than monthly. The worst part is the guilt of not contributing to the household in the way I did in the past, and sometimes asking my husband for money. It is humbling.

I seem to have lost my former self-confidence and self-esteem. I don't feel capable. I feel "less than," inadequate and inferior. I am tentative. I keep second guessing myself. I have noticed that I am keeping my head down, because I do not feel whole. And while I have such wonderful support around me, I feel isolated, small, and insignificant. I keep telling myself that this condition is temporary, given time I will reclaim my mojo. I am counting on this.

I have felt the different stages of grief for myself: grief and denial as I lament the loss of the familiar; anger and guilt, as though I had caused the cancer; and depression because my life will never be the same again.

I keep asking myself, "How am I supposed to behave as a cancer patient?" I am looking for a playbook that tells me that this is the face of the poster child of cancer, but I can't find anything. This is an individual journey. Part of me wants to have nothing to do with it, to deny its existence, to scream for someone to make my body normal again. Another part of me wants to battle this beast. Moment by moment, I vacillate between feeling sorry for myself, getting sad and angry, and bracing myself for the long journey ahead.

It took me two months of introspection before I found my answer. And the answer was to surrender to God's will. Rather than controlling and forcing life to unfold as I wanted it to, I needed to accept with grace what has happened to me. This acceptance came slowly as I sorted out my feelings, talked to others, learned more about the cancer, and figured out what was in my control.

From this place of submission, I am reshaping my identity, keeping the important parts intact and exploring who I will be during this time. I am not only going to tolerate my condition, I am going to embrace it. I am not going to wait the cancers out; I am going to live. I have started to make a mental list of all the things I want to do but have not had the time for: luxuries, like sleeping in and reading. And I'm going to use this time to grow, to become better in every aspect of my life. It's weird and counter-intuitive but cancer is giving me a new beginning.

Cancer is just a word and does not need to define us. We may not like the word but we get to choose how that word is applied to our life.

Watching Her Go Through Her Losses— Sabrina

Many of us need to remain active to feel alive, to feel that we are worth something. Our minds churn with thoughts of upcoming tasks; our desks are scattered with to-do lists; and we get caught up in routine as the years pass by. Our productivity is measured by the amount we accomplish each day, and before even completing the last sentence of an email, our attention has already shifted to what's next on our list. Even after work, we run from this birthday party to that wedding reception; laundry, cooking, and cleaning squeeze their way in between. We long for all-inclusive beach vacations as an opportunity to put away our smartphones and take a moment to breathe. As a society, our drive for efficiency and instant results forces us to become compulsive doers.

My mom personifies this philosophy. As an organizational development and leadership guru, she has constantly been on the move, working for a range of retail, pharmaceutical, financial, insurance, health care, and government organizations for over thirty years. I have always thought of her as Mary Poppins incarnate—arriving at a company with gusto, causing transformational change and making a meaningful impact before moving on to another organization.

Then came the cancer diagnosis. Over the past months, much of what has defined her as a person—and arguably, provided her self-worth—has been radically shaken. No longer is her success determined by something grand, such as implementing a company-wide change model, but rather it is determined by accomplishing something that was once instinctive but is no longer that—like the ability to jump out of bed and put on a pot of tea, or climb a flight of stairs without assistance. Her condition has forced her to embrace the art of simply being. Pre-cancer, my mom would stand up from the table with the last bite of her dinner still on her plate, scarfing it down on her way to the sink, and rushing to her next task. Or she would be watching a television show with me in the living room, while speaking on the phone with someone else and putting on nail polish, all at the same time. She was an epic multitasker. Recently, I've noticed her slow down and be more mindful of every moment. What brings her pleasure now is something as simple as the ability to taste food to its last bite; or to listen to music; or watch a good movie uninterrupted. She's more patient, especially with people, taking the extra few minutes to listen rather than jumping in right away with advice.

My mom has had to learn to listen to her body. She has had to become conscious of where she will spend the limited amount of energy she has. She has had to learn to accept and trust that everything will be okay. She continues to take on projects around the house with enthusiasm when she has energy, like cleaning the garage or organizing the contents of the kitchen cupboards. But by balancing the doing with just being, she has allowed space for new priorities to emerge and to explore a new way of living.

Uncooperative Veins

Chemo treatment for non-Hodgkin lymphoma is difficult for my body to handle. The standard treatment, which I am undergoing, consists of six treatments known as R-CHOP that take place once every three weeks. R-CHOP is an acronym that stands for five medications:

Rituximab (Rituxan)
Cyclophosphamide
doxorubicin Hydrochloride
vincristine (Oncovin, Vincasar PFS)
Prednisone

These medications are delivered orally and intravenously over a full-day stay in a ward known as chemo day care in the hospital. The side-effects can be severe and range from those I have been told to expect—anemia, nausea, diarrhea, hair loss, tiredness, sore mouth, discolored urine, stomach issues, loss of appetite, neuropathy, rapid weight loss and gain—to more serious side ones like febrile neutropenia (high fever with infection of the blood), which will require hospitalization, and reduced hemoglobin and platelets, which will require transfusions.

During my R-CHOP treatments, I ended up in the emergency ward of the hospital seven times, with overnight stays of a total of twenty-eight days. With little warning, my body would become extremely hot, my limbs would shake, and I would develop a high fever. This was especially distressing, because we would have taken every precaution to avoid fevers and infections, and I was determined *not* to go to the hospital if I could help it. Not to receive multiple needle pokes in my arms for blood samples, and saline-solution and drug injections into my near-dead or nonexistent veins. Not to be in a hospital ward once again and remain isolated from the world that I loved so much.

At the hospital, I would have an ECG, a chest X-ray, numerous blood and urine tests, and, of course, the requisite IV to distribute antibiotics quickly into my body. Over time my veins would not tolerate the constant IV insertions and simply refused to cooperate. The nurses would struggle, heading for this spot then that one, going through every inch of my arm. One nurse would give up and another take up the fight. They might find a vein finally and briskly start to draw blood—and then exclaim in annoyance as the flow stopped abruptly. "It was just there," I would hear, and agree. It was just there. They would go to my other arm with even more resolve, searching, probing, pushing. They tried putting heat on the arm, slapping it, asking me to make a fist. The veins played Houdini and simply kept disappearing. Then the intrepid nurses would try one of the larger veins in one leg. It was uncomfortable and I would yell with pain. After consultations, the medical team finally decided that a central line would be the best option for me. The central line is a catheter inserted into a large vein in the neck close to the heart, and is used to administer both fluids and medications.

Typically the central line is inserted in a different department of the hospital by specialized technicians, but since there was a backlog of patients and I needed my daily dose of antibiotics, the attending physician informed me that his residents would do the job right there, under his supervision. He was supremely confident that it could be done quickly and effortlessly and asked Nagib and Sabrina to leave the room and return in twenty minutes. Lying on the bed with a sheet over my face, I felt stabs of pain shooting down my neck and heard the faint murmurs of the frustrated physician as his residents tried poke after poke with no success. I felt like a corpse—a collection of skin and bones that medical students were experimenting on. A Frankenstein monster. The physician stepped in, his anxiety obviously increasing with every failed attempt. His ego was certainly taking a beating. It was on his ninth try, after almost ninety minutes, that he was finally able to locate a vein and insert the line. After the procedure, there was no apology for putting me through the experience. In fact, he seemed visibly frustrated with me for making his job more difficult, as if I had a choice in the matter. This was an unusual experience; all my other doctors had been kind.

For days, I sported the marks on my neck to show the attempted and failed insertions. The central line was useful for one day and then removed for a PICC line (peripherally inserted central catheter) the very next day. I occasionally shudder when I think of the one-day central-line debacle. I wonder if the doctor has given it any thought.

Love You Forever—Sabrina

April 20, 2012

When I was a little girl, I would sneak into my parents' bed every morning and cuddle up to my mom before starting the day. And though I am a grown-up now, I still find every opportunity I can to cuddle my mom whenever I'm home. We are self-acclaimed cuddling superstars.

But yesterday, our cuddling was different. I held my mom in a bed at Toronto General Hospital while she was shaking from an intense fever. I cradled her in my arms as tightly as I could and rubbed my arms against her back, her legs, kissed her head, anything to make her chills go away.

As I held her, I thought about one of our favorite childhood books, *Love You Forever* by Robert Munsch. In the story, a mother spent her entire life looking after her son. Whether he was a teething two-year-old, a hormone-driven teenager, or a grown man, she would sneak into his bedroom at night, cradle him in her arms and sing: "I'll love you forever, I'll like you for always. As long as I'm living, my baby you'll be." And this went on until one day she became too old and frail to be able to do it anymore. And so the boy held his mother in his arms and sang to her: "I'll love you forever, I'll like you for always. As long as I'm living, my Mommy you'll be."

My mom has held me through everything—more times than I can say. But yesterday, it was my turn to hold her, to keep her warm, to keep her safe, to tell her everything would be okay. It's tough, seeing someone you love suffer—and feeling like the only thing you can do is hold her for dear life, praying her cancers will go away.

When her fever finally broke, and she had kicked off the five blankets covering her, she immediately snapped into mom-mode and asked me about my dinner date, coached me through my work and talked to me about the importance of leaving a legacy. I have seen these cancers make my mom weak and vulnerable. I have held her hand as the disease has stripped her of her hair. I have watched the pounds fall off her. But what they haven't done is touch her spirit, the stuff that makes her who she is. If anything, these cancers have made her even stronger, more certain, more beautiful.

As I sit here at Schiphol Airport in Amsterdam waiting to board a flight to Nairobi, Kenya to finish up some work commitments, my heart aches to be with my mom. I'll be back in Toronto in two weeks where I can hold my mom again and say, "I'll love you forever, I'll like you for always. As long as I'm living, my Mommy you'll be."

Life Feels Different—Shayne

The last few months, since my mom's diagnosis, have been difficult. Life feels very different these days. I still wake up every morning, put on a suit and tie and rush into the office with a coffee in hand. But there is a certain heaviness that I carry around. The realization that someone you love is suffering so intensely, while your family is struggling to cope during the most difficult of times; the fear that your mom—the person who you go to for advice and cheers on every one of your successes—may not be around for much longer. Should I quit my promising career and spend more time at home? Should I propose to my girlfriend of two years so that my mom can witness her son getting married?

I've been spending more time at work these days. My manager and colleagues have been supportive ("if you ever need to leave the office, just go, don't ask")—but I've found the best way to deal with this life-altering event is to bury my head in work. I have always been an expert in compartmentalizing, a skill I aptly learned from my mom. It's easy to do when you're in a challenging job that requires your full attention, but there are times when it doesn't work so well. I was at the bar near my office on a recent Friday evening, sitting with a few colleagues who were trading stories about the latest mergers and acquisitions they were working on.

"I was doing one last check of the Board presentation at 1 AM when I noticed that he didn't deduct interest expense from the accretion dilution analysis! That's Finance 101!"

"I can't believe we hired him. So what did you do? Did you call him back to the office?"

I broke up the complaining with a humble request: "Guys, can we talk about something other than work?" My associates looked surprised. What could be more interesting than gossiping about colleagues and bragging about how many hours you worked that week? To tell you the truth, I was a guilty participant. When you are working more than seventy hours a week, there is something strangely therapeutic about walking down to the bar on a Friday night, lost in a sea of expensive suits and designer handbags, and gossiping with colleagues. But the last few months have felt different. When friends talk about work, sports, or even the trials and tribulations of their love lives, I often sit there quietly. Sometimes, I just want to stand on a table and yell, "Why do you care so much about such trivial things? Don't you know my mom is dying?" Other times, I just want to excuse myself and leave, and go home to be around my family.

The other night I was stuck at work, finishing yet another urgent assignment. My mom had been admitted to hospital with a case of febrile neutropenia. I really wanted to see her that night, so I snuck away from the office around 10 PM and headed to the hospital. Visiting hours were over but no one noticed as I tiptoed by the nurses' station and followed the signs to her room. My mom was already asleep. I put the bouquet of flowers that I had picked up from the hospital gift shop in a vase and sat by her bed, careful not to make a sound. I put my hand on hers. Her face was puffy, her veins were bruised, but she looked peaceful in this moment. It's hard to compartmentalize when the very thing you're trying to compartmentalize is lying in a hospital bed right in front of you. I probably shouldn't quit my job, I thought. There's no way I could do this every day.

When Legs Don't Work

The evening started out well. I was feeling strong and decided impulsively to go to jamatkhana for prayers. With so many hospital stays, I hadn't been able to go as regularly as I would have liked. Going to jamatkhana is important to me, for praying and meeting all the people there, who are like my family. This evening I wore my new purple lipstick and sported my new leather, black-laced boots with a side zipper and a one-inch heel. I wore my shoes proudly, having worn only flats for a whole year. I felt tall and confident. The parking lot was full, so I parked my car at a lot close by. As I was walking towards the jamatkhana, my legs suddenly gave way and buckled under me. I fell to the ground. My immediate thought was, "No big deal, I just need to get up." Only, I could not. I had no strength in my legs, and try as I would, I could not lift myself up. I thought about calling Nagib. I thought about calling someone in the jamatkhana to tell them where I was and ask for help. My purse, with my phone, had fallen a few feet away and I was not able to reach it.

It was dark and I felt completely alone. The reality of my condition, how helpless I had become, how my body had abandoned me hit me hard. I started to cry. Oh God, what has become of me? How could someone so able, so competent, be reduced to this? What have I become? I examined my legs and saw bruises, blood, and dirt, as I waited for someone to arrive at the same lot and find me. "Please, God, help me," I begged.

The poem "Footprints in the Sand" came to mind. God whispers, "My precious child, I love you and will never leave you . . . When you saw only one set of footprints, it was then that I carried you." Fighting back tears, I waited for what seemed like a very long time, until a woman saw me and came rushing towards me. She tried to lift me up but couldn't. I was dead weight. She told me she would get help and to stay where I was. The irony in her comment—or was she being funny to make me feel better?—struck me, but I was too tired to respond. Within minutes, a volunteer from the jamatkhana came by, lifted me up, and walked me slowly to the building.

When I came home that evening, I didn't tell Nagib what had happened. He found out a few days later from someone at jamatkhana and came home fuming. My husband is overly protective, and I've tried my best to respect his need to take care of me. It's his way of having some semblance of control over a situation we didn't choose to be in. But sometimes I don't want to feel like a cancer patient or an invalid. I don't want to wait for others to help me. I don't want to seek permission to do some normal activity, like going for prayers. Pre-cancer, I was fiercely independent, and it scares me that I may never be so again. The scars on my legs from that fall are a potent reminder that I may never be.

Perspective—Sabrina

Nine days. Three types of drugs. Eight different nurses. Five collapsed veins. Twenty-plus needle pokes.

This past week has been a tough one for my mom. She had another fever at home on Sunday night, and we rushed her to the emergency department at Toronto General Hospital. Since she seems to be getting febrile neutropenia a lot between her chemo treatments, Dr Tiedemann has given us strict orders that any sign of a high temperature requires an immediate visit to the hospital. Her immune system is low, her body is weak. It has been a roller coaster ride of low blood pressure, antibiotics, antivirals, antifungals, and another dangerously low hemoglobin level of 59, and I'm afraid one day her body will say "enough."

When the hospital becomes your home, when you are surrounded by beeping machines, animated neighbors, and medical and body smells, it is easy to get discouraged. But there is immense value in taking a step back.

If we take a few million steps back to East Africa and think about the health-care system there, it certainly puts things into perspective. I recently returned from a two-week trip to Kenya to wrap up my work contract. I'll be in Toronto taking care of my mom now for however long she needs me. While I was away, I facilitated a workshop with nurses in a rural district in Kenya to understand the challenges they face. For many, it takes over an hour to reach the dispensary. They travel on foot and when they arrive, they are greeted by a long queue of people who woke up at dawn and also walked a long distance to seek attention. The quality of care the nurses are able to give is limited by drug shortages and poor equipment. There is never enough staff—one or two nurses manage the clinical, administrative, and financial components of their facility by themselves. They are constrained by time, money, equipment, and cultural practices. The words *not enough* and *lack of* were often heard. And in a rural community, *not enough* and *lack of* equate to the loss of livelihood, the loss of economic sufficiency, and often the loss of life.

The last nine days have been rough. I have watched my mom's temperature and blood pressure fluctuate constantly, and I cannot help but imagine what would happen if my mom were being treated in one of the health facilities I have frequented in rural East Africa. There would have been no nurse available to monitor her vitals every hour and administer the medications she needed to get better—the shortage of nurses (38 nurses for a population of 100,000) would have made this impossible.

For the last nine days, I have sung to my mom as technicians drew her blood to check her white blood cell and neutrophil counts for the day. As hard as it is to see her cry, I know that if we were in rural East Africa, it would take days to get the results of simple blood tests like these—only a few facilities have laboratory services.

For the last nine days, I have triple-checked the antibodies listed for the blood being transfused to my mom. But if we were in a rural East African district, the likelihood of blood being in stock for an emergency transfusion is highly questionable. And a well-matched blood cross-checked for three different antibodies would have been impossible to find.

This past week was a tough one, but it could have been a lot worse. And as I watch my mom sit on our backyard deck today, minus IVs, enjoying the sunshine, so happy to be home, I feel a sense of gratitude and hope that all will be well.

More Perspective

June 1, 2012

After a nine-day stay in hospital for febrile neutropenia, I've come home. For a day. Tomorrow I must return to the hospital for a bone-marrow biopsy and a CT scan. I feel that I practically live at the hospital these days. I have mixed feelings about long hospital stays. On the one hand I am grateful to know that I am in the best possible place to be taken care of by nurses and doctors, particularly when I am feeling so fatigued and can hardly look after myself. It gives me a place to sleep and I convince myself that my being in the hospital takes away the burden from my family and gives them a welcome break from having to take care of me. I am not sure they agree. I tell myself I'm used to it, but I'm not. When will it end? End, not with my death but with me cured. I don't know when, and I don't know *if*.

The results of the biopsy will be available in two weeks and will show whether the lymphoma "has been knocked down," to quote Dr Tiedemann. He says, in his delightful Kiwi accent, that he is "very confident."

Me? I am cautiously hopeful.

But at the same time, the third chemo and the subsequent blood transfusion are taking their toll. I am experiencing all the side effects of chemo at the same time, and I feel like a cancer patient. The symptoms include extreme fatigue, fever, constipation (resulting in hemorrhoids—ouch), mouth sores that make it difficult to eat and talk, zero appetite, and a change in taste sensations. The fatigue is the most debilitating.

Since the chemo drugs lower my immune system's ability to fight off viruses and bacteria, I've been advised to stay away from large gatherings of people. On chemo days, I live in a cocoon, withdrawn and alone on the living room couch, covered in a red and orange striped Masai blanket that Sabrina brought for me from Kenya—until Nagib comes home.

On these chemo days, just the thought of getting out of bed, getting dressed, brushing my teeth, and going downstairs for breakfast tires me out. I want to hide under the covers and sleep all day. It's like being in the land of the living dead, a zombie, not available to anyone. My family is seeing me helpless, weak, and unresponsive. This is as difficult for them as it is for me.

But I don't mean for this to be about me. I want to write about a lady who was in the bed beside me in the emergency room last week. Imagine a thirty-something blonde, pretty, with beautiful eyes but looking a bit gaunt. For an hour and a half she was on the phone, anxiously trying to find someone who could pick up her eleven-year-old daughter from a friend's place and look after her while she was in the hospital. During each call, she had to repeat her story and cried. Finally she found someone who would care for her daughter, and I heard the relief in her voice and a deep sigh. My heart went out to this woman.

As we waited overnight in a shared room in emergency, I got to know this young woman. Her name was Leslie. She had been waiting for a liver transplant for the past two years, meanwhile she came to the hospital daily at 1 PM to "clean" her liver. This time she had to stay, since she had developed a blood infection.

She had three children, eleven, four, and three years old. She was a single mother. Every weekday she drove to a subway station near her home, then took a train to the hospital for her treatment. Then, despite feeling nauseous, she forced herself back onto the subway and rushed to get to her car so she could pick up her kids. This was her regimen every day. She knew that she could not continue it indefinitely. I tried to have her think about support and resources that she could tap into, so she could focus on getting better. I also gave her the contact information of someone who could help her. I hope she followed through. I never asked her about the father of the three children.

I have thought of Leslie every day this week and have marveled at how strong she is—stronger than I could ever be. I think about how she looks after her three young children even though she is so sick and has to be in the hospital every day. I think of how depressing it would be to have to wait for a liver transplant for two years, with no imminent hope of getting one. When I reflect on her situation, I realize how lucky I am.

Yes, I have two cancers. I also have a definite treatment plan with a time frame and an oncologist who is optimistic that I will beat the cancers. And I have a wonderful network of support from my family and friends. Central to this is Nagib, who has held me with gentleness, compassion, and deep love throughout.

What I have learned from meeting Leslie is that if you look outside your bubble and take the time to look at the people around you, there is much to discover. Everyone has their story. And while you may think your situation is dire, there are people whose challenges are greater. It's all about perspective.

A Fortuitous Event—Sabrina

June 10, 2012

My mom has many loves in her life—her husband of thirty years, Cadbury Whole Nut chocolate bars, trips to Florida, and most recently, avocados, a new craving. But above all else, she has an unrelenting, unwavering, unquestionable love for the Toronto Blue Jays. Impossible as it may seem, that love hit an all-time high this week.

After three days of up-and-down temperatures, followed by consistent spells of fever and fatigue, she finally agreed to be taken to the hospital. On auto-pilot, we packed her bag, reached TGH, and made our way through the familiar routes of triage and registration. As we were settling into her room in the emergency ward, we heard the most awful noise coming from the room next door. An older man had been brought in by paramedics and was screaming in pain. He did not speak English and the nurses were having trouble understanding him. Soon a well-dressed, dark-skinned, tall, muscular Dominican man passed our open door and entered that patient's room. Mom and I looked at each other in disbelief.

"No!"

"That couldn't be?"

"Could it?"

"Was that really him?"

"Impossible!"

Our suspicions were confirmed when we overheard a doctor enter our neighbor's room and introduce himself as the doctor of the Toronto Blue Jays. Edwin Encarnacion—the Jays' first baseman and home-run hitter extraordinaire—was actually less than ten steps away from us. Swoon.

Star-struck, we put my mom's fever on the back burner and began deliberating a plan of attack. Mom saw this coincidence as a sign of incredible good fortune and was convinced we needed to profess our love for the man. Or at least say hello. I wanted to err on the side of caution and not bother Edwin (clearly, we were on first-name basis now). After all, he had come to see his father. Nevertheless, for a solid half hour, we forgot about fevers and cancers and strategized. We thought about buying Lettieri's infamous hot chocolates and maybe slipping one into his room with our number on it. The cleaning lady had left her mop and bucket in the hallway, and though I am not domesticated by any means, the thought crossed our minds to do a little cleaning in our neighbor's room. We even flirted with the idea of walking through the door separating our two rooms and "accidentally" stumbling across Edwin Encarnacion—with our best looks of surprise, of course. We shamelessly Googled his latest stats and learned some pick-up lines in Spanish in case an opportunity presented itself to use them.

Alas, before we could execute any of these plans, the nurse ordered some tests and my mom grudgingly complied and was wheeled to the testing room. As we made our way back from the tests, there was the dashing, twenty-nine-year old Dominican heartthrob on his cell phone right outside our room. Urine bottle in one hand and my hand in the other, my mom said to him, "You're Edwin Encarnacion, right?" He acknowledged us with a nod, looking preoccupied. But a few moments later my mom called out his name as he walked by and he came into our room. She told him we watched every Jays game and how much we adored him, how we loved when he came up to bat, and then again, how much we loved him, and a few oh-my-gods, followed by prayers for his dad to get better soon. I stared. Perhaps a bit too longingly. Edwin was incredibly gracious (and incredibly gorgeous) and said thank you a number of times before leaving the room. He acknowledged us with a wave the next time he passed our room and I wished him a good game that night when he later walked past me in the hall to leave the hospital. He did have two hits that evening and made a fantastic diving catch. We take a little bit of credit for this, given the stream of compliments Mom threw his way.

My mom is still in hospital with a case of low hemoglobin and neutrophil counts, but since laying her eyes on the great Edwin Encarnacion, she has yet to have a fever. Lesson learned: the best cure for febrile neutropenia is meeting a superstar celeb!

Darkness Before Dawn—Nagib

June 11, 2012

It was a dark night indeed. I woke up with a sense of dread. Muni's body was extremely hot and her limbs were shaking.

"Oh, no!" I said. "This isn't supposed to happen." How can she have a fever now? After every precaution we've taken? Five injections of Neupogen to promote white cell production, 3,000 mg of Valacyclovir daily to prevent infections. No going out, no visitors during the "dip," when her neutrophil numbers are down and she is most vulnerable to getting sick.

But a fever she had. Initially 38.7° Celsius and then, despite two Tylenols, 39.5°. Throughout the day, she continued to fight fevers and fought to *not* go to the hospital. Finally, after the Blue Jays had thrashed Shayne's beloved Atlanta Braves 12-4, and after Lewis Hamilton had won the Canadian Grand Prix, and when 4,000 mg of Extra Strength Tylenol were not doing their job, she agreed to go to the hospital.

Within a couple of hours, Muni had been poked and prodded at Toronto General's emergency department, seen by the now-familiar nurses and doctors and diagnosed for the third time with febrile neutropenia, a condition where the neutrophil blood cells are low, and anemia, a condition where the red blood-cell count is low. Muni's white blood cell count was zero, and her red blood-cell count was just 68. No wonder she was fighting a fever and was dizzyingly fatigued.

Shayne and Sabrina showed up just in time, since by now my head was throbbing from the tension. And, as our kids are wont to do, they livened up the atmosphere and sent me back home.

Overnight, I was thinking: could it be that the chemo drugs have knocked down all the bad cells and are now zeroing in on all the good cells? Or is the cancer so aggressive that we are losing the battle? We will have to wait until later this week to see Dr Tiedemann about the results of the bone-marrow biopsy.

You've heard the expression that it is darkest before dawn. That was certainly true for me then.

Sabrina stayed up all night with Muni. Just as the blood transfusion was finished, Muni's cell phone rang. It was Dr Tiedemann.

"Oh no!" said Sabrina. "Why is he calling today? Is there a problem?"

"Mrs Premji," he said, "I have some good news for you. I have reviewed the bone-marrow test results, and *there is no sign of lymphoma. And the myeloma cells have reduced as well.* I know you've had a rough few days but wanted to give you this news today instead of waiting until next week."

Yay! The lymphoma had been beaten and the multiple myeloma had been knocked back. We said *shukran tasbih* (prayers of thanks) and then celebrated with grape popsicles.

We still had some way to go. We needed to get Muni out of the hospital, then deal with her further treatments for myeloma. But we were on the right path.

As I left Toronto General Hospital for the night, I couldn't help but notice a sign posted in the lobby. In bold letters, it read "Cancer can be beaten." I smiled, thinking, "Cancer has been beaten."

A Roller Coaster Ride

June 24, 2012

The last three weeks have been a bit of a roller coaster. First, we got the incredible news that the lymphoma is in remission. I continue to pinch myself, savoring the news. I have one more chemo tomorrow after which Dr Tiedemann will do another bone-marrow test and confirm that the lymphoma has, in fact, completely been eradicated from my body.

Dr Tiedemann gave us the news of the remission while I was in the hospital for febrile neutropenia, a result of my chemotherapy. I ended up staying in the hospital for seven long days, requiring three blood transfusions. For the entire time that it took each unit of blood to enter my body, I would pray for the people who donated the matching blood that was keeping me alive. Getting out of bed was tough; even going to the bathroom required effort. All I wanted to do was sleep. And sleep I did, until my hemoglobin count went up and I could start functioning again.

There are always gifts to find in the hospital: I met a vibrant woman, Wannietta Prescod, who was in hospital for reconstructive surgery after having beaten breast cancer. Wannietta was a school bus driver and three-time champion of Canada's Search for the Fastest Knitter. She had a personal best of 245 stitches in three minutes, and she came third in the world at the '08 Knit Out. She presented me with a beautiful scarf that she had knitted while in the bed beside mine.

Tiredness has become my constant companion. I have lost strength in my legs and climbing stairs has become a challenge. I've had two falls since coming home from the hospital. Thankfully, nothing's broken. My current goal is to walk around the park next to my home where I have met a couple of regulars, a Chinese woman in her 80s who walks around the neighborhood with gusto three times a day, and a tall, good-looking, vibrant East Asian couple who exercise in the park together and carry a yellow sun umbrella. I have befriended them and shared my cancer story with them. They have offered to meet me in the park every day to walk with me, insisting that I allow them to hold their big umbrella over me to protect me from the sun.

It is wonderful to be home again, embraced by the love of my family. And as I reflect on the past few weeks, I give thanks that the lymphoma is in remission. I give thanks to the extraordinary care I have received that gives me a fighting chance. I give thanks to all those who have sent messages of support and love and prayers. Even though I haven't been able to respond, I am truly humbled and grateful. As Nagib once said, "Your prayers are like a tide that has lifted us in these stormy seas."

I Rang the Bell!

June 26, 2012

The Princess Margaret Cancer Centre has a wonderful tradition. Once a patient has completed the full course of chemotherapy treatments, she gets to ring the Bravery Bell. Today, after my sixth and final R-CHOP chemotherapy treatment had ended, I rang that bell with gusto—so loud that I am sure it could be heard all around the world.

For my family and me, it marked the culmination of nearly four months of chemo treatments for my lymphoma. It began on March 12, and at times during the treatment I felt like I was in hell. The side effects were anemia, nausea, diarrhea, hair loss, tiredness, sore mouth, loss of appetite, neuropathy, rapid weight loss and gain, blood transfusions and frequent infections that required hospitalization. The bell was a symbol of courage, hope, and a new beginning. Nagib made this a celebratory event and brought *Prairie Girl* cupcakes for all the nurses and volunteers who were present, who had given of their time to say hello, make my stay comfortable, provided juices, snacks, and newspapers and sometimes offered a shoulder to cry on or a recipe to try.

At Princess Margaret, as with any hospital, nurses are the cogs that make the wheels go round. Manuel Martinez was one such nurse. Manny was a bit of a legend at chemo day care. I first heard about Manny from a colleague whose husband was treated there. I heard about him again on my first day of chemo when a nurse said that Manny had the magic touch and would be able to find my elusive vein for the IVs. I heard about him in the chemo waiting area where patients were hoping that Manny would be assigned to them. I finally met him at my second chemo session. He was my nurse for a brief period and I wished he could be my nurse for each appointment.

Manny has earned his reputation. He has worked at Princess Margaret for some twenty years. In 2010, he was nominated by a patient for the Toronto Star Nightingale Award, an award for outstanding service. He has also been nominated eight times for the hospital's Gerald Kirsh Humanitarian Award, winning it in 2007. What strikes me most about him is his quick wit and his ability to tell wonderful stories. He is so completely patient-focused that when he is your nurse, you can leave all your anxieties behind. You are in competent hands. His gift is his ability to see you as a person, not just a patient. Manny is one of many wonderful nurses who support the chemo ward at the hospital. There are 15 to 18 nurses who look after approximately 655 patients per week. Today was my last chemo for the lymphoma and it was only fitting that Manny was my nurse.

This chemo was the easiest I have experienced because there was no long search for uncooperative veins, no pokes for blood, no IVs. I was so relaxed that I slept through the entire treatment. Why did I not get the PICC line earlier?

We are still smiling after this battle with lymphoma. We still have to get the myeloma beaten. But now the Premji family can enter the next phase of our journey where the attention will be on dealing with the multiple myeloma. We are curious about what Dr Tiedemann has in mind for the treatment. We will find out in the next couple of weeks.

Reflections on the Past Six Months

August 1, 2012

It has been six long months since I was diagnosed with non-Hodgkin lymphoma. To celebrate the end of my treatment for this cancer, Nagib, Sabrina, and I took a one-week vacation to St Pete Beach, Florida. Shayne was busy at work and couldn't join us. When we last came here eleven years ago, our suitcases were filled with sport gadgets and toys—baseball gloves, frisbees, and beach balls. It was a magical, uncomplicated time, when we spent hours building sandcastles and playing on the beach. This time our kids were adults and our suitcases looked quite different.

There were the prescribed medications, alcohol swabs, bandages, and syringes with saline and heparin that Nagib would need to administer to me so that my PICC line would remain open for the requisite blood work and the chemo for myeloma, my other cancer, upon my return. My suitcase boasted three wigs that I planned to wear on date nights. I had also packed my blue, Seal-Tight cover for the PICC line so that I could shower and keep the line clear and dry.

I started to think about the suitcase as a metaphor for life. What is it that we each carry? What baggage? What items that serve us well? Is our suitcase overflowing with things that bring us joy? Or does it take away from what makes us happy? I suppose that at different stages of life, we may need different things in our suitcase. Every so often, we may need to pack and unpack, and make choices about what is important to us.

Florida gave me a lot of time to think about my life with cancer. I worried about the odds against me, about the quality of my life, about my family, about the future. Worry shows up in my brain like an uninvited guest. I find it annoying and unconstructive. I can see how it robs me of strength. And often, it's unnecessary because things get resolved as they will—whether I worry or not. As we were driving to Fort De Soto Beach, listed as one of the top ten beaches in the US, I saw a bus that had the following bumper sticker: "Relax, God's in Charge!" I laughed hard when I read this; it was almost as if God was sending me a personal message: Quit worrying.

One of my favorite authors, Stephen Covey, in his book *The 7 Habits of Highly Effective People*, talks about the Circle of Influence versus the Circle of Concern. His message is that effective people focus their energy on things they can influence; this enables them to be proactive, solution-driven, and purposeful. Ineffective people tend to waste their time concerned about things they have no control over and therefore cannot do anything about.

I think we all crave a certain amount of control over our destiny. When life throws a curve ball—or two—it can feel like things are spinning out of control at a dizzying pace. And yet, here, in the midst of all the uncertainty I was facing, I found that there were a lot of things I could influence. I could choose how to react and respond to the cancer and the treatments. I could be thankful that the lymphoma was in remission. I could be optimistic about the upcoming treatment for the multiple myeloma. I could visualize the good cells fighting and getting rid of the cancer cells.

I believe that we are in partnership with God. We cannot sit back and let him do all the work. We have to do our part and trust that He knows what is best. It's only human to worry. But it's also liberating to know that God is the architect, the master planner, the director, and the producer.

So I have set aside my worrying and found a solution that works for me. It is a symbolic God's Box, modeled on one that a friend told me about. Hers is a small, unassuming red box that she has had for four years. Each time she feels overwhelmed, she writes down her anxiety, worry, request, or insecurity and puts it in the box for God. She tells me that the sheer act of writing out her worries helps her unburden herself and sometimes even gives her clarity. Periodically, she will go through her God's Box. Each time she has found that every worry she put in her box has been resolved; some within a day, some in a month; some in a year. For her, this is a testament of faith, of knowing that there is a higher presence.

I am inspired by my friend's story and have created my own version of God's Box. Each night, I talk to God about four things: what I am grateful for that day, people in my thoughts, magical moments, and stuff I need God's help with. This week, for instance, I expressed my gratitude for being in Florida and being able to taste and eat different foods. I prayed for people I know who are ill, for two who died this week and for all the children in the world. On another night, I thanked God for the magical moments I can enjoy, I told Him about dancing with Nagib at a Cuban restaurant while the singer caressed us with his version of "Unchained Melody." I also asked for help as I told Him how nervous I was to start treatment for myeloma next week. It took all of five minutes, and I cannot think of a better way to end the day. It is my sacred time with God and it is a date I keep every night.

Ending Before You Begin

I am a huge believer in the philosophy that you must end something before you begin again; our vacation to Florida gave us just the opportunity for this. It was the midpoint of my cancer treatments. The lymphoma was in remission and I would be starting treatment for multiple myeloma in two weeks. So Florida gave us the occasion to celebrate, to reflect, and to recharge. We stayed at a hotel overlooking the water in St Pete Beach. We woke up with the sun. We swam, we walked, we talked, we watched beautiful sunsets.

And we ate. After months of not being able to enjoy or taste most foods, my appetite had come back with a vengeance. I enjoyed crabs and blackened fish at Crabby Bill's, consumed huge portions of pasta and salad, experimented with Thai and Cuban food, and wolfed down waffles with all sorts of toppings from the Waffle House. I will never take food for granted again. I put on much-needed weight and my stomach was happy with me.

I wore different wigs every day. On our last day, I chose not to wear a wig. While we were checking out, the staff at reception started to chuckle and one of them remarked that finally things were making sense. She explained that every night they thought they were seeing Nagib with a different woman, and therefore they had nicknamed him Casanova. Now, seeing me bald, they realized that there was only one woman, but with different hairstyles. We laughed all the way to the airport and I teased Nagib mercilessly with his new name. Casanova!

We landed back in Toronto on August 1, and my chemo began the next day. Florida was the perfect place to close Part One of this journey and we welcomed Part Two with optimism and a sense of moving forward.

To Life!—Sabrina

Since my mom's diagnosis, it has become our family tradition to propose a toast with every drink. Whether it's a virgin strawberry daiquiri, fresh lemonade at Fort De Soto Beach, or coffee at Denny's, our toast is always the same—to life. I'm not sure how it started, but it is a ritual that has become very meaningful for us. For each one of us, it symbolizes something different. My dad sees the alternative of life as death; toasting to life is a reminder that his life partner is alive and well, that my mom is still with us in spite of two severe blood cancers. My mom lives and breathes our toasts—for her, it captures a moment to celebrate being alive. So, as I sit here on the beach with the starry night above me and the sound of the ocean all around, I would like to propose a toast to life.

Here's to the certainty of the sun rising every day and the stars shining every night.

To surprises, unexpected delights, and all the joy that comes our way.

To confidence as we move in the direction of our dreams.

To experience; to the joy of being present.

To first dates, play dates, and everything in-between.

To laughter.

To exclamation marks!

To freedom, to choice, to being the hero of your own story.

To unexpected curveballs and roadblocks with a bag of lessons to be learned.

To time—every second, every moment of it.

To first sips and last bites.

To the beauty of our dreams, and the magic of making them come true.

To love, the greatest of all forces, and holding onto it once we've been lucky enough to find it.

To family and to friends who find their way into our hearts.

To a world of opportunity and living in the world of possibilities.

To hope, and to the courage and faith to know that everything will be okay.

To the gift of living; to each breath.

For this is what life is. To life!

3.

MULTIPLE MYELOMA

Myeloma at a Glance

What Is Multiple Myeloma?

Multiple mycloma, or myeloma, is a cancer that begins in the plasma cells. Plasma cells are found in the bone marrow. The buildup of plasma cells in the bone marrow causes a depletion of normal cells there, weakened bones, tumors, and infections. The cause of multiple mycloma is not known and there is no cure at this time. The goal of the treatment is to reduce symptoms and slow the progression of the disease.

Myeloma Statistics

According to 2019 data from the Canadian Cancer Society, there are approximately 3,300 new cases of multiple myeloma each year and approximately 1,550 Canadians will die from multiple myeloma in 2019. The five-year survival rate for myeloma is 44% (the ten-year survival rate is 32%).

Symptoms

Symptoms and signs of multiple myeloma include anemia, bone tenderness, bone pain, weakness in the body, bone fractures, kidney damage, nerve damage, skin lesions, recurrent infections, extreme thirst, and frequent urination.

Treatment

Treatment options for multiple myeloma include chemotherapy, radiation therapy, surgery, stem-cell transplants, and drugs to manage the immune system. In some cases, a wait-and-watch approach is taken.

Source:
> https://www.myelomacanada.ca/
> https://www.cancer.ca

My Encounter with Myeloma

August-October 2012

It takes numerous tests to determine if you have myeloma. These begin with X-rays, CT scans, and MRIs, a complete blood profile, a protein electrophoresis, bone-marrow biopsies, a skeletal bone survey, a PET scan, an electrocardiogram, and a pulmonary function test. After all these tests, I was diagnosed with IgG kappa multiple myeloma, Stage 3. I remember thinking "It could be worse. It could be Stage 4," until I realized that there was no Stage 4.

A few years ago, the prognosis for myeloma patients was dismal. More recently, however, treatments have helped patients extend their lives, sometimes for many years. When I was first diagnosed, my oncologist, Dr Tiedemann, indicated that the median survival rate was approximately five years after treatment. But it is possible to survive for more than ten years. At the current rate of progress, we will hopefully have found a permanent cure for this cancer by then. But in order to do this, scientists must figure out the cause of the cancer.

My treatment for multiple myeloma includes 12 to 16 weekly rounds of the chemotherapy cocktail CYBORD, a combination of oral and intravenous chemicals and steroids. Neupogen injections are administered to stimulate the growth of white cells in the body prior to chemotherapy, and an infusion of pamidronate every month is taken to reduce the risks of broken bones and bone pain.

This chemo is quite different from the one I received for the non-Hodgkin lymphoma. Every week, during the period of this treatment, I will have to take twenty-two pills at home on the day of the chemo, go to the hospital for blood work, and finally check in at chemo day care to receive more medication through IV-infusion. The IV medication is Bortezomib, a drug sold under the name Velcade. It is a new and highly effective drug for treating myeloma, a proteasome inhibitor that takes about ten seconds to administer. The drug is not currently covered by the Ontario provincial government for all cases and the cost of each dose is approximately $3,000; I will need to pay a total of $48,000 for the four months of my treatment. Dr Tiedemann has submitted a request to the distributor of the drug in Canada to approve it for me on compassionate grounds. The possibility that the drug company might not approve the drug loomed in the back of our minds every day and we alternated between hoping and praying for a break. It was a stressful time as we considered different options in the event that I was not approved. On our last day in Florida, we got the welcome news from the drug company via phone confirming that they would cover the cost. We were elated, because this meant that we would not be out of pocket.

One of the main components of the CYBORD cocktail is Dexamethasone, or Dexa. It is critically important, because it has been shown to kill cancer cells. It also reduces swelling and inflammation. I love the feeling I get when I get my 40 mg of Dexa every Friday. I am brilliant on Dexa and can solve *Wheel of Fortune* puzzles with only two or three letters on the board. I also can't sleep through the night and use the time to solve the world's problems. Dexa gives me a glimpse of the old, pre-cancer me—fearless, confident, loud, feisty, spontaneous, and resourceful.

The problem is that this state lasts for about three days, and then comes the crash. It is not pretty—mood swings, tiredness, sadness, preferring to sit in a corner without speaking to anyone. And then like an addict I crave for the coming Friday to get my next dose. It is truly a love/hate relationship and probably not very healthy, as Dexa is known to have long-term side effects that include bone loss and heart and eyesight problems.

Dexa affects not just me but my family too, often in unexpected ways. Sometimes the energy spike lets us do normal things like going to a movie or grocery-shopping. But because I can't predict when I will get the high, there can be interesting—and sometimes hilarious—consequences. Once I vacuumed the entire house at 3 AM; another time I cleaned out the garage, lifting heavy boxes and attacking decades of junk in mighty swoops. My worst moment was when Nagib woke up in the middle of the night to go to the bathroom; only to find me, when he returned, stripping the bed and putting new sheets on. One week, while high on Dexa, I interviewed for a volunteer position to manage a leadership project. I proceeded to tell the interviewer passionately why the project would not work in the way it was presented and what needed to change for it to be successful. I don't think I let her get a word in edgewise. Needless to say, I did not get the job.

My family has had to tread carefully when I am on my Dexa high. I get opinionated, aggressive, loud, and impatient. I remember how surprised I was when I heard Nagib complain to Dr Tiedemann about how tough it was to live with me during my Dexa treatments. He has a video of me belting out the *Jersey Boys* soundtrack during a chemo session, while he is doing his best to contain me, knowing that other patients in the room, some of them newly diagnosed with cancer, were having a hard time coping with the news and treatment. I am trying hard to find a way to become more self-aware while on Dexa to preserve my relationship with Nagib, while at the same time using the Dexa super-energy to power through projects with brilliance and clarity.

The doctor heard Nagib, and when I went for my next chemo, he had split my Dexa dose over two days. I've noticed the difference: my energy is more contained, I am able to sleep a few hours at night, and the crash is more bearable.

Welcome to life on the treatment train.

Labels Are for Jars, Not for People

September 6, 2012

Something delightful happened to me when I went for chemo treatment today. It was a beautiful day and I woke up happy. I paid particular attention to how I dressed. I decided to wear a skirt with an oversized top and a colorful scarf. I even applied purple nail polish. When I got to the hospital, I was mistaken for a visitor, and not a cancer patient!

I was astounded. Each time I have gone to the hospital, ever since my first diagnosis on February 3, my identity has been that of a cancer patient. When I got my weekly blood work done, my hospital number was checked and I was asked to confirm my name and date of birth. When I went to the chemo ward, I met with the same routine. I was first and foremost a patient and was treated as such. And I responded by acting like a patient—passive, acquiescing, obeying. This was easy to do when I was not feeling particularly well. But I have decided to change the dance. I have started dressing up for my hospital visits and looking forward to them. I am finding that, as a result, I am walking taller and taking charge.

I went to the hospital today with the intention of making the hours-long visit work for me and the people who looked after me. I wanted to focus on getting to know the people behind the uniforms. The curious thing is that when I changed my dance, the people I interacted with were compelled to change their rhythm too. My relationships with my caregivers at the hospital transformed—from just talking about my cancer to richer conversations about what is going on in our lives. Manny told me how he had proposed to his girlfriend. Samina wanted to serve the community. Tennyson was thrilled to be with her four grandchildren. Astrid had traveling to Africa on his bucket list.

When I was assigned to my chemo pod, there was a cancer patient seated beside me who thought I was a visitor and asked me which patient I was here with. I was flabbergasted, and then overjoyed. And it came to me that we often label people and limit them to the constraints of that label. We are all so much more than that. Each of us is a fascinating, complex being with hopes, dreams, challenges, pain, passion, and stories. What if we stopped labeling each other? What if we got curious about everyone we meet—even our parents, children, and significant others—as though we were meeting them for the first time? What might we discover, what might we create together? Labels are for jars, not for people!

"God Could Not Be Everywhere, So He Created Mothers."—Sabrina

September 11, 2012

Recently, a good friend's mother passed away after a three-and-a-half-year battle with breast cancer. When I heard the news, I immediately snuck into my mom's bed and held her tight, watching her chest move up and down with every breath—thankful that she was alive.

Someone once said, "God could not be everywhere, so He created mothers," and I could not agree more. Moms are truly special. They have arms that were made for holding, for cradling, for loving. In the past twenty-four years, my mom has used her arms to tuck me in every night, to rub my injured back, to wax my legs for the first time, to make her infamous tacos when my friends came over, to comfort me after a bad day, to hold my hand before I crossed security at the airport, to squeeze me tight when I needed TLC, to love me unconditionally. As I grew older and bigger, there was always more than enough room to fit into my mom's arms. She's a magician.

As God's special agents, mothers are armed with ears to listen non-judgmentally and mouths to say the right thing. They are given eyes that can see past the brave faces, past the mistakes, past the insecurities and hearts that know no bounds. They juggle a million things at a time, wearing different hats throughout the day and they still go to bed with smiles on their faces.

Yesterday, while listening to my friend talk about his mom's passing,

I came to realize that a mother's real superpower is the way she lives on long after she's left this world. Her legacy is maintained through the people she touched in her life and through her children. In the values her children espouse and the people they grow up to be. In every decision, in every tough choice they have to make, she is there. At every holiday, at every time of celebration, she is there. She is always there. And when her children have children of their own, and tell stories about their grandmother, she becomes alive again and her legacy continues. That's the true power of a mother.

From hearing of my friend's mom's death, due to our own family experience this year, and through many other stories we have heard about people and their journeys with cancer, it has never been more apparent how fragile life is. How important it is not to take things for granted. How essential it is to make the most of every moment we have with those who give meaning to our lives, to learn from them, to show our love, to carry their legacies forward.

My mom is an extraordinary woman. And although there is currently no cure for multiple myeloma, with God's grace she will have many more years to create a bigger dent in the universe.

Fading Away

September 15, 2012

In the past week, I have started experiencing another side effect of my treatment, known as "chemo brain." It's not so good—frightening, really. I had read about how chemotherapy results in a feeling that the brain is in a fog, and that patients experience difficulties with memory loss. As the cumulative effects of the drugs pile on, I notice that it's taking me a little longer to process information, something I was really good at during pre-cancer days. In addition, I am having trouble with concentrating, with multitasking, and with remembering.

This past week, the fog has been all-encompassing. I went to my bedroom to get something, but could not remember what it was. I searched the recesses of my brain and the more I rifled through it, the more elusive was the memory. I decided to write a blog post as a distraction and could not remember how to access the blog site on the computer. And when driving to the hospital for an appointment, I made a couple of wrong turns and ended up in a strange part of town. When I finally made it to the hospital, I had trouble remembering whether to get off the elevator on the third or the fourth floor. And I was mixing up words (the other day I said backdraw, instead of drawback). This is a big blow to my identity and how I see myself.

I am scared. I hear that this is not a permanent condition. But what if it is? Nagib values competence above all else, and a big part of our

Saturday morning breakfast dates are long and delicious conversations about politics, religion, social issues, business, sports, life. What if I am no longer able to participate; what will that do to our relationship? Shayne and Sabrina are constantly sending me articles to read and links of podcasts to listen to. I can't process the information easily and can't recall it when they ask me for my opinion. "I don't remember" is becoming a part of my new vocabulary, and I am not liking it. Actually, I am hating it.

Is this how I want to live? Is this how I want to be remembered? Will it get any better? What is the quality of life when my memory is fading away? My plan is to have a conversation with my family about end-of-life decisions if the situation warrants it.

Once You Choose Hope, Anything Is Possible

September/October, 2012

In late September, after I had gone through eight weekly treatments of CYBORD for multiple myeloma, Nagib and I took off to Niagara for the weekend to enjoy the fall scenery. As the leaves changed color, and farmers' markets filled with barrels of apples, tomatoes, and red-hot chili peppers, I was anticipating a transformation of my own. My attention shifted to the next part of the treatment, which consisted of stem-cell mobilization, collection, and transplant and would take place later in October. There was a lot of information to take in. I had been told that prior to the stem-cell transplant, I would receive an aggressive dose of cyclophosphamide—four times the strength I had been getting so far in my chemotherapy treatments, to prepare me for the upcoming transplant. I had also been warned that I would receive daily injections of Neupogen in my stomach to stimulate the bone marrow to produce more stem cells and release them into the bloodstream. At some point I would need to get a Hickman line inserted into my chest—a catheter used to infuse the stem cells into my body.

I went to the hospital feeling nervous about the new chemotherapy and the start of the stem-cell process. I checked into the chemo day care reception on the fourth floor and asked the receptionist for one of the limited number of beds in the unit instead of a chair, and also requested that my favorite nurse, Manny, look after me. She said she would do her best. It turned out that there were no beds available. We made our way to Orange Pod, Chair No 23, and as we rounded a corner, we were greeted with a familiar face that came like a ray of sunshine: Manny!

As soon as he saw us, he opened his arms to give Nagib, Sabrina, and me a giant bear hug. He told us how excited he was that I was starting the stem-cell process, how lucky I was to be selected for the transplant (because not everyone is, it all depends on the severity of their condition), and how today was the first day of the rest of my life. Suddenly, I went from being overwhelmed to feeling hopeful. It took an incredibly empathetic nurse to offer us a different perspective and to show me that there could be another way of looking at my situation.

It was a long day at the hospital, but Manny provided phenomenal care, and made us laugh with his stories and funny quips. He presented me with a beautiful silver bracelet that said, "Once you CHOOSE HOPE, anything is possible." Coincidentally, I had been reflecting on the word *hope* these past few days and had come upon the realization about the profound need for hope in our lives.

As we go through life, we face many challenges. They may be at work or in relationships. They may be questions about life and spirituality, or concerns about family and children. Health issues can take up a lot of our time and effort. We each find our different ways to deal with these challenges. We might keep a positive attitude, while looking for opportunities in the midst of the challenges; we might turn to prayer, or talk to a friend, or decide how to spend our money and energy; we might make some decisions—good or bad. For me, the common ground of these disparate strategies is hope. Without it, one wouldn't try any of them.

And when there is hope—even a glimmer of it—people find a way through. When there is hope, there is optimism and resourcefulness. Hope allows us to make choices and decisions. In the absence of hope, there is nothing to look forward to, and giving up—and giving in— follows. Once you choose hope, anything is indeed possible.

Stem-cell Mobilization

October 5, 2012

After the chemotherapy, I started the process for stem-cell mobilization, ie the collection and reinfusion of my stem cells. I've been given drugs that cause my stem cells to move from my bone marrow into my bloodstream. They will then be harvested from my blood, stored, and transplanted back into my body when enough have been collected.

What are stem cells anyway? Stem cells are partially developed cells that can fully develop into over 200 different types of specialized cells, such as nerve cells, muscle cells, liver cells, and red blood cells. Myeloma occurs when there is an overproduction of plasma cells in the bone marrow, as a result of which they crowd out and suppress other cells, including red blood cells (which carry oxygen to the organs in the body), white blood cells (which help to fight infection), and platelets (which help to form blood clots to prevent prolonged bleeding).

Stem-cell collection is a fascinating process. First, a simple blood test determines whether there are enough stem cells circulating in the bloodstream. Approximately two million stem cells per kilogram of a patient's weight are required. If there are not enough stem cells in my body, I will have to continue with the Neupogen injections and keep returning to the hospital every day for a blood test until there are enough stem cells to harvest. For most patients, this can usually be done within two to three days.

The stem cells are collected through a Quinton line, which is a plastic tube surgically inserted into a large vein in the neck. The technique for collecting stem cells from the bloodstream is known as apheresis. A cell separator device (the apheresis machine) collects blood through the Quinton line, separates the stem cells which are collected in a small bag attached to the machine, and returns the remaining blood back into the body through the existing PICC line in my left forearm.

Each session takes approximately four to five hours, and may be repeated for two to five days until sufficient stem cells have been collected for two transplants. When this occurs, the Quinton line is removed and I go home to wait. The stem cells, light pink in color, are frozen until it is time to transplant them into my body.

As there are only a limited number of transplant beds available in the hospital, with many patients awaiting their stem-cell or bone-marrow transplants, I may have to wait for up to two months. In the meantime, I may begin a third cycle of weekly chemotherapy treatments (each cycle is four weeks) and I will undergo a battery of tests: a dental exam (by oncology dental specialists), another pulmonary function test (to assess the functioning of my lungs), a MUGA scan (X-rays of the heart), and an echocardiogram (ultrasound of the heart). These tests ensure that my organs are functioning well and provide a baseline for measuring the changes that may occur after the transplant.

In a couple of weeks, I'm scheduled for a minor surgical procedure to insert a Hickman line (a catheter into a large vein in the chest below the collarbone). It is the most secure method to administer chemotherapy, draw blood, and reinfuse the stem cells into the blood stream. My PICC line, which has served me faithfully for four months, through thick and thin, at home and on vacation, in and out of water, will be removed at this time.

The stem-cell transplantation process begins with admission into the hospital as soon as I get "the call." On day one, a high dose of melphalan (another, even more powerful chemotherapy drug) is infused, in order to wipe out all the red and white blood cells and platelets in my bone marrow. On day two, the transplant doctor brings back my frozen stem cells and thaws them in a warm water bath. Once thawed, the cells are reinfused through my Hickman line, much like a blood transfusion.

I'm told that once the stem cells are infused, I will smell like creamed corn for 24 to 48 hours. This is because the chemical used to preserve and protect my cells during the freezing process (dimethyl sulfoxide) smells like corn. Then it's up to my transplanted stem cells to "engraft," ie to begin to grow and produce new, cancer-free cells. This entire process will require me to stay in hospital for up to three weeks, during which time I may require additional blood transfusions. By December, I look forward to coming home transformed into a new—albeit tired—Munira Premji, all bundled up and ready to tackle the cold and snow of the winter season.

When Things Don't Work Out

October 16, 2012

I arrived at Princess Margaret at 7 AM. A sample of my blood was taken, and it appeared that there might be enough stem cells to begin harvesting. I was hooked up to the apheresis machine, ready and excited to begin this next stage of the therapy. Every hour, Nagib, Sabrina, and I kept sneaking glances at the precious little bag attached to the machine that would indicate how many stem cells were collected. Unfortunately, the bag remained empty, and I was given an injection of Neupogen to stimulate the stem cells and told to come back the next day.

On day 2, we were back at the hospital at 7 AM and the process was tried again. After six grueling hours, my eyes fixed on the stem-cell collection bag, the nurses called it quits and I was disconnected from the machine. Karen, the lead nurse, said that this sometimes happened and the following day would be better. She injected me with Neupogen in my stomach to stimulate the production of blood cells and sent me home.

Day 3 did not yield any results. This was not good news. Meanwhile other patients were getting their stem cells collected. I had another Neupogen injection in the stomach and was sent home. A Neupogen injection costs about $350, and I was quickly becoming an expensive liability to the health system.

On the morning of Day 4, the alarm clock interrupted me from happy dreams. I woke up Nagib and told him that today would be the day—I had a good feeling. We drove to the hospital, making our usual breakfast stop at Tim Hortons. I checked into the stem-cell unit for my routine pre-treatment blood draw. The nurse at the counter recognized me, smiled, and called me by name. She took my blood and said, "Fingers crossed." Rather than connect me to the apheresis machine right away, the team decided to analyze my blood. An hour later, the nurse came back to say that they didn't see enough stem cells showing up in my system; so, no collection.

On Day 5, we went back to the hospital, with renewed vigor. More pokes. More pre-blood work. More anxious waiting. The nurse came to the waiting room an hour later and shook her head.

On Day 6, we made the trek back to the hospital. Same results. No collection. Now I was envious of the other patients there who got their stem cells harvested so easily.

Day 7. More blood work, with a dose of positivity from the nurses not to give up. Unfortunately, my stem cells were not listening. There were so many bruises on my stomach from Neupogen injections that Karen had some difficulty finding a spot to insert the needle. Finally she found it, and we left the hospital, feeling deflated.

On Day 8, our optimism was fading and we were in a seriously worried frame of mind. More pokes. More blood work. No collection.

Without the stem cells, I would not have the transplant, and this would directly impact how long I had to live. I felt I was letting everybody down. Friends and family kept telling me to stay positive, but my body was whispering to me something else. "I am tired." "I am weary." "I am giving up."

Our hopes were fading, and we were scheduled to see Dr Tiedemann in a few days to figure out what happens next and come up with an alternate plan if necessary.

Strange Dreams

October 20, 2012

This past week I have seen my husband go through the depths of despair. Being a caregiver is not easy, and Nagib is having to go through more than can be reasonably expected. And while he does an incredible job of protecting and taking care of me, this week I perceive him carrying the burden of this in his mind, in his body, in his being. There is the look of hopelessness and bleakness in the way he carries himself. He tries to be strong but I see the gloom envelope him. He is eerily quiet. My heart weeps for Nagib but I don't know what to say. I hold him, and he pushes me away.

I can't help but reflect on a dream I had earlier this week. I am in conversation with six or seven women to determine who would be the best fit for Nagib after I have passed on. I talk to them about the extraordinary man he is, about his gentle soul, about his razor-sharp smarts, about his goodness, about his mantra of patience and moderation. I want to find out who will make his heart soar, who will laugh with him, who will be his best friend. I am not allowing myself to feel anything because I am resolute in my goal of finding Nagib that special person.

Somewhere in the dream, I make a commitment that I am not going to die at home, because it would be awful for Nagib if he started his new life with a new partner in the same home where I took my last breath. I feel myself going deeper and deeper in the abyss of this dream that I can't wake up from. I will myself out of my panicked state and wake up with a giant headache.

I often wonder what will happen to Nagib when I die. I want him to move on with his life and learn to love again. I have thought of broaching this subject with him, but can't find the words.

Setback or a Speed Bump?

October 27, 2012

We had an appointment with Dr Tiedemann last week and he discussed the progress of the treatments so far. Dr Tiedemann looked grim and expressed concern.

In spite of the two months of chemotherapy, the multiple myeloma has not decreased as much as he would have liked. He is looking for at least a ninety percent remission, or even a hundred, before continuing with a stem-cell transplant. He performed another bone-marrow aspiration and biopsy on me to get an accurate reading on the number of myeloma cells in my bone marrow. Based on the results of the biopsy, he will likely recommend another two cycles of chemotherapy with Velcade or another drug. This will probably take all of November and December. Once the cancer is eliminated by ninety percent or more, I will have to go through the stem-cell mobilization and collection process all over again. If everything goes well, this should take place in January and February of next year.

We left the hospital feeling quite deflated. We hadn't expected this setback. In our minds, the myeloma would be wiped out after two months of targeted chemotherapy. I would have a stem-cell transplant in November and spend most of December in hospital recovering. We had talked hopefully about closing the chapter on cancer by the end of this year. Now it looked like it would take longer.

This was when the doubts started to pile up. What if the chemotherapy did not work? What if my body was not able to handle the constant assault of the drugs? What if Dr Tiedemann concluded that I was not a good candidate for a stem-cell transplant? We thought through my situation over the next few days. We went to jamatkhana daily and prayed. All this introspection and discussion of our fears caused us to rethink our expectations and count our blessings.

First, instead of fretting over having two cancers simultaneously, we thanked God for an unexpected blessing. The chemotherapy treatments for the lymphoma had not only defeated it but also knocked down the multiple myeloma by fifty percent. Further, the chemotherapy treatments for the myeloma reduced the M-proteins to 17 grams per liter. This is considered, in medical terms, a partial response, better than stable disease (no change) or refractory disease (an increase in M-proteins). Our goal was to get a very good partial response (ninety percent remission) or a complete response (hundred percent remission).

In the end, we strengthened our resolve to beat this cancer and not let it hamper our plans. We decided to stop calling this a setback—it was just a speed bump on our journey through cancer.

A Secret Love Affair—Sabrina

November 11, 2012

This past Tuesday, my parents sat cuddled on the couch tuned in to CNN's election night coverage. With their prediction sheets in hand, they shared insights about US politics, debated passionately, and marked off states for the Democrats and Republicans as the votes swirled in. Although Mom had been arguably the biggest follower of the election in our family over the last few weeks, her attention was strangely divided this night. Part of her heart was entangled with my dad's, part of it was love-struck by Barack Obama; but the largest part of her attention was focused on a large, juicy orange.

I wish I were joking but I have caught my mom in this predicament a number of times recently. She has ditched my dad at bedtime for an orange; her face has lit up, not at the sight of me but at the bag of oranges in my hands after grocery shopping. She has been late for lunch dates because she has indulged in an orange before leaving the house. My mom is officially in a love affair with oranges.

Oranges have not been my mom's only tease over the last few months. Since starting chemotherapy, she has engaged in intense relationships with Cadbury Whole Nut chocolate, pina colada milkshakes, chocolate chip ice cream, sour cream and onion potato chips, hot dogs, popcorn, and most recently hot and sour soup, and sushi.

Her relationship with food over the course of her treatment has been interesting to observe. Foods she once craved are now intolerable, scorned lovers that have been relegated to outcast status. Foods she had disliked for years have suddenly piqued her interest and our grocery bill. Mealtimes in our home are full of surprises.

Cancer can be a difficult journey. But when I catch my mom in the living room at midnight devouring an orange, juice flowing down her chin and arms, her face a complete mess, I can only sit back and laugh.

You Get What You Focus On

The school of cancer forces you to come to terms with how you live with the illness. I knew that I didn't want to be a whiner, complaining incessantly about how unfair life is. I did not want to be a victim, grasping my needy hands around my family. I did not want to live my days in self-absorbed self-pity. The game changer for me was when I stopped thinking about what I didn't want and started to think about how I wanted to live in the midst of my illness. I shifted my focus and made a commitment to living fully, with vitality and intention, in a way that felt true to me.

Yes, I have weekly hospital visits, chemo treatments, side effects to contend with, blood transfusions. I have tough days. I am aware of the reality of my situation and what I'm up against. But I don't focus on it. I accept these as things that need to be done and then I move on. I don't fight them or get mad about them. Cancer is a part of my life now, but one that I choose not to give too much energy or attention to. This has allowed me the bandwidth to focus on things that matter to me.

I think of focus as a flashlight. When we aim our flashlight at something, that's where our energy will flow. Energy flows where attention goes. I stopped focusing my energy on feeling sorry for myself, on endless hospital visits and long waits, on painful procedures. Instead I shifted my energy on what I wanted more of—precious moments with

117

the family, savoring a meal, energy to take a walk on the boardwalk.

I have also discovered the value of the affirmations that have become a part of my healing. Several times a day, I will make one or more of these affirmations to strengthen my focus:

- Every cell in my body sings with energy and vitality.
- My body heals quickly and easily.
- I accept and embrace my cancer.
- I am whole. I am complete. I am Munira.
- I can choose my response to any situation.
- Each day is a new opportunity.
- Today is the first day of the rest of my life.
- I am a divine expression of a loving God.
- My body will harvest enough stem cells for the transplant to happen.

Popping like Popcorn

Dejected and hopeless, we made our way to Dr Tiedemann's office to figure out the next steps in my treatment. Should we still try to harvest stem cells, even though my body perversely refuses to yield them? Should we consider a different treatment? Should we continue with more chemo?

Dr Tiedemann informed us that Mozobil, a drug manufactured by the French pharmaceutical company Sanofi, would be the best chance to boost my stem-cell harvest. Unfortunately, I did not meet the criteria for Mozobil, because it is only available to patients as a second-line treatment (ie when the initial treatment doesn't work). As wonderful as Canada's health care system is, drug affordability is an issue that many patients continue to face. Typically, new drugs are offered for free by the manufacturer. Once the drug has been proven to be effective, manufacturers stop giving it for free and it is up to the insurance companies to pick up the tab. Often there is a time lag before the insurers agree to pay for the drug. My treatment happens to lie in this lag period, meaning that we would need to find a way to cover the cost of the drug.

After some research, I was disheartened to learn that Mozobil cost $12,000 a vial, and I would need three vials. We did not have $36,000 sitting around. Nagib insisted that we go to the bank immediately and get a line of credit for these funds. I remember arguing with him that

I was living on borrowed time anyway, the Mozobil might or might not work, and maybe it was time to reevaluate the need for a stem-cell transplant for me. Deep down I knew that there was no hope for me without this procedure; I needed to have my cells collected and harvested, and without Mozobil there was no chance of making that happen. I was an emotional wreck and feeling guilty for putting my family through yet another hurdle. I remember Nagib telling me, "It's only money; I would pay a million dollars for each day that I get to spend with you."

The next day, in a Hail Mary attempt, I called JoAnne Langshaw, my boss at Sanofi, where I happened to be working as an HR consultant at the time. I told her I needed Mozobil and asked if I could get it at a reduced price. "Let me see what I can do," she responded. JoAnne spoke to Mark Lievonen, the president of Sanofi Canada, who contacted the manufacturers in Laval, Quebec. Within two weeks, through a series of fortuitous connections where business leaders put humanity over profit, three vials of Mozobil were delivered to Princess Margaret Cancer Care, at zero cost to me. I'm particularly grateful to JoAnne Langshaw, Mark Lievonen, and Jill Forsythe, the key account manager of oncology based in Laval, who made the case that, "we're in the business of saving lives and we have one of our own who needs this drug."

When I went to pick up the Mozobil at the Princess Margaret, the pharmacist was almost giddy with excitement, this being her first exposure to the drug. I suppose she knew that it had the potential to extend life. I marveled at how small each vial was.

On December 10, 2012, Nagib injected me with the Mozobil in my stomach at 10:40 PM. His hands were shaking, my heart was pounding, and my mom was praying loudly. We went to the hospital the next morning, our ninth time, with renewed hope. I cannot begin to describe the emotions that flooded our hearts as the nurse took the blood samples from me to determine if today was going to be my lucky day. Would they be able to find a vein to pull out blood? Would enough stem cells be detected? Would they send us home disappointed yet once again? Could we take any more of this?

After what seemed like an eternity, but was no more than thirty minutes, we received the good news. We could start the stem-cell collection immediately! The nurses worked efficiently to get me ready. They connected me to an apheresis machine using two ends of tubing. For six hours, blood flowed out of my arm and through the tubing to a centrifuge where it was spun at high speed. The spinning separated the blood into different components. The stem-cell layer would be collected in a bag and the remaining blood returned to me via my other arm. We watched the bag anxiously to see how many stem cells, if any, was being oozed into it. Normally there should be enough for two transplants; I would have been happy if enough were collected for one.

Through the magic of Mozobil, my stem cells woke up and started collecting into the little bag, inch by inch. The head nurse kept coming by to check the progress. She was cautious at the beginning, not to show too much enthusiasm, but then we saw her steps lighten and her smile get bigger. She refused to say anything to us just yet, until finally, when she was certain, she whispered in my ear that they were able to collect enough stem cells, not just for one transplant, but for two! All the nurses in the unit did a dance; I wept and Sabrina brought a cupcake to celebrate.

The magic of Mozobil continued beyond me. Since I only needed one vial to collect enough stem cells, the other vials went to two other patients, who benefitted from them.

My stem cells will stay frozen at the hospital until a bed becomes available, which can be anywhere from two to eight weeks. Until then, I plan to cozy up by the fireplace and bid farewell to this unexpected year and ring in a new one.

When I Grow Up, I Want to Be My Mom— Sabrina

January 1, 2013

We rang in the new year in the emergency department of Toronto General Hospital. Unfortunately, Mom had another attack of febrile neutropenia the previous night. I was at a New Year's party at a friend's place when my dad sent the message that they were on their way to the hospital. Mom was quickly triaged and I arrived just in time to cuddle her into 2013, as Dad played auld lang syne on his phone, singing animatedly along.

New beginnings are opportunities to set resolutions, but gym memberships and dieting seem trivial this year. What I really want, I've decided, is to be like my mom.

Over the past year, I have watched her grapple with the toughest news she has ever had to receive. I have overheard her discussions with friends describing the day she was diagnosed and her treatment to date—no pretension, no victim attitude, simply real and honest conversations. I admire her honesty, her ability to feel the good and the bad intensely and to embrace the vulnerability of her situation.

With each curve ball my mom has been thrown—a second cancer diagnosis, blood transfusions, acute hyper hemolytic anemia——she has stepped up to the plate confidently and hit it out of the park. She has approached uncertainty with positivity and resilience. She is fighting her cancers with every ounce of energy she can muster. And thus she has shown me what a gift it is to be alive. Her will to fight has demonstrated to me that life is much too precious to give up easily. This has been a particularly important message for me as I've been battling my own demons this year and have, on several occasions, struggled with the desire to continue to live. It's hard watching the person you love most in this world disappear in front of your eyes. I've never had close friends beyond my mom, and the thought has crossed my mind a number of times this year that I could lose her. My mom's infectious energy has always set the tone in our family. Lately she's been exhausted and sad, and it makes us all hyper-concerned. And then I see my dad, whose every breath revolves around my mom's health. This past year, he has been in a perpetual state of worry. He doesn't have a support network beyond my mom and me, and I don't know how to take care of them both. I hadn't realized how much of a toll being a primary caregiver takes on your sanity.

No matter how fatigued and drained my mom is, it's impressive that she still finds a way to show that every day, every moment is one worth living fully. Her finely manicured toenails, impeccably clean Toyota RAV4, and enviable sense of style are proof that cancer does not have to interrupt living.

As difficult as it has been putting my life on pause and moving back to Toronto, it has been a joy to be home and spend time watching my mom, learning from her, trying to emulate her ways. I crave our time together, whether on our drives to the hospital, waiting anxiously for test results, or sharing a killer milkshake at the Pickle Barrel. These precious moments are opportunities for my mom to share her thoughts with me. She speaks about the importance of appreciating the little things in life—nurses who can find her vein right away, blood draws that don't hurt, waking up in the morning with an appetite. She has made me promise to enjoy every bite of food—something she has struggled with after chemotherapy. She shows me that it is important to take the time to celebrate the small stuff, because it's the small stuff that makes this ride worthwhile.

Faced with two late-stage cancers, it would be easy to drown in a pool of self-pity and ask, "Why me?" But instead, by asking the more empowering question of "Where is the learning in this?" my mom has taught me the value of perspective. You can make virtually any situation a positive one simply by changing your paradigm—looking at it another way.

My mom may have cancer, but when she walks into the hospital, she looks like a supermodel. Business suit, heeled boots, funky jewelry—this is the new look of a woman with cancer, and hopefully soon, a cancer survivor. My mom went so far as to call my dad and me bums for wearing jeans to her last appointment—and we have dressed to the nines ever since. She has taught me that no matter what experience comes your way, good or bad, you tackle it head on with confidence, with flair, and with style.

That's my mom. A stylish, radiant woman with an extraordinary spirit and an unbelievable zest for life. Even in her worst of times, she is a role model, showing me the importance of living each day as if it were your last.

Slow Down—Nagib

January 31, 2013

Yesterday, the media was buzzing with news about the long-awaited launch of the new Blackberry. Last year, Blackberry-maker RIM made a strategic decision not to rush to market with an incomplete product, but to slow down. Slow down, and make sure the final product would work well and last a long time. They were criticized for delaying the launch, but they were resolute in their decision.

An editorial in the *Globe and Mail* newspaper applauded them for this:

> In a world where customers and stock markets are relent-less in their demand for constant innovation, RIM has done something strikingly original: It has taken its time.

Of course, in hindsight, perhaps they were too slow to market and should have acted sooner. Or maybe, they should have waited a little longer still and developed a stronger product to compete against Apple.

At the time, I thought that our experience with Munira's cancer in the last few months had been similar to Blackberry's. Since Munira was diagnosed with multiple myeloma in 2012, we had been focused on fixing her (with chemotherapy and stem-cell transplants) and relaunching the brand-new, cancer-free Munira, version 2.0. Initially the plan was to have her complete her chemotherapy and stem-cell transplants within six months, but due to the further diagnosis of lymphoma, that plan had to be set aside until the lymphoma was put into remission. So it was with great anticipation that we came back from our much-needed one-week vacation in Florida to begin treatments for the multiple myeloma. Weekly chemotherapy treatments started as planned in August and continued for twelve weeks, during which time Munira suffered severe side effects from CYBORD (Cyclophosphomate, Bortezomib, and Dexamethasone—Dexa!). But she endured, knowing that this therapy had been proven to slow down multiple myeloma. When that happened, her body would be ready for a stem-cell transplant.

You have to know this about Munira—she is impatient at the best of times. Her "Red Energy" requires her to be doing something constantly. She doesn't know the meaning of slowing down, and she certainly can't stand delays. But in the medical system, there are always delays. The first such delay in her case was the process of collecting stem cells, known as apheresis. The process did not work completely, despite nine daily trips to the hospital and numerous Neupogen injections. Thankfully, Mozobil, Sanofi's wonder drug, came to the rescue, and on December 11, 2012, we were able to collect enough stem cells for multiple transplants, if necessary. Now the waiting game began: we had to wait for a bed to become available in the stem-cell transplant unit at the Princess Margaret Cancer Centre.

Through the Christmas holidays and into the new year, the unit remained extremely busy; patients who were expected to be discharged became sick, and the waiting list grew. We were told that our wait would be anywhere from two to eight weeks. Munira was not ready to stand by and wait. She made repeated calls to every possible medical professional, begging and pleading with them, but she couldn't "pull a Muni," a phrase we use to describe her remarkable ability to make seemingly impossible things happen. This time though, she had to wait.

In the meantime, her weekly chemotherapy treatments were restarted on January 12—Dr Tiedemann didn't want her to go too long without treatment while she was waiting for a transplant. But we noticed that some of the symptoms of the lymphoma (such as night sweats) were returning. Out of an abundance of caution, Dr Tiedemann ordered a

CT scan of all the lymph nodes; happily, they came back negative for any abnormal activity.

Then, yesterday, with anticipation, we sat down with Dr Tiedemann and waited for him to say, "Pack your bags, you are all set to be admitted for the stem-cell transplant." Instead, he expressed concern over the night sweats and ordered further tests, including yet another bone-marrow aspiration and biopsy. We needed to wait two more weeks to rule out definitively any recurrence of lymphoma.

My mantra through life has been "patience and moderation." I was completely on board with Dr Tiedemann's plan, but Munira would not be convinced. "We have waited so long for this," she said. "And the biopsies are excruciatingly painful." She just wanted to get it over with and, you know, get on with life.

That's when I showed her the *Globe and Mail* editorial. Like Blackberry's stakeholders, we had to make the tough decision to take the time and do it right. Finally she agreed that an additional two- or three-week delay in the transplant process was, in the scheme of things, a relatively short period of time. We decided to slow down and do it right.

And so over the next two weeks, Munira has decided to live life even more fully (her weekly chemotherapy will continue). Last week, we went to 5th Element, an Indian fusion restaurant on Queen Street West, for her birthday. The food was so delicious that she invited the chef home to teach her how to cook new Indian dishes. We have also both joined GoodLife Fitness, to keep physically fit and strong for the three-week long hospital stay and the two- to three-month long recovery period at home that will follow the transplant.

In gratitude for accepting my suggestion of the slower and steadier path, I bought her the new Blackberry Z10 to keep her busy and engaged, as she will have lots of time on her hands over the next few months. Munira is an iPad and iPod junkie, so it will be interesting to see if her alliances change with the new Blackberry Z10.

For now, though, slow and steady will hopefully win the race.

The Stem-cell Transplant Process—It's Finally Happening

On the morning of Wednesday, February 13, I got a call that a bed had become available and I needed to get to the hospital immediately for my stem-cell transplant. I had waited so long for this news that when it came, tears just rolled down my face.

Coincidentally, when I got the call, I was already at the hospital for an appointment with Dr Tiedemann. He confirmed that the bone-marrow biopsy taken two weeks ago had come back negative for lymphoma and the plasma cells in my bone marrow had been reduced by 90 percent. He smiled when he told us that the multiple myeloma had been significantly knocked down and that it was transplant time. I was so happy that I gave Dr Tiedemann an enormous hug.

We rushed home and packed my bags. In addition to the normal stuff one would take to the hospital, I took with me two wigs and five lipsticks. Such vanity!

The first day of my hospital stay was rather uneventful, as it involved sleeping in a strange bed and waiting for something to happen. Today, the second day and Valentine's Day, started with a flurry of activity. I was woken up at 5 AM for blood work, following which I had an ECG and a chest X-ray. My next-door neighbor, Judy, was undergoing a similar routine and remarked, "With all this activity, the day will be over by nine!"

I was seen by Dr Norman Franke in the stem-cell transplant unit. Dr Franke's reputation had preceded him—he was a doctor beloved by those who had had transplants. A wiry man with gray hair and a twinkle in his eye, he was humble, articulate, funny, and very easy to talk to. His was a well-functioning unit and he gave credit for this to his exemplary staff. He gave me a calendar for the three weeks I was expected to be in the hospital and painted an honest picture of what to expect. It would be a roller coaster.

Nagib showed up with a bouquet of roses for Valentine's Day and had to keep telling all who stopped him that they were artificial (live plants, flowers, fruits, and vegetables were not permitted in the unit). I was touched by this simple gesture of love and it filled my heart with love and gratitude.

At 11 AM, I was given melphalan, a high-dose chemotherapy drug, to kill the remaining myeloma cells in my bone marrow and decrease the amount of abnormal blood protein produced by them. I think of melphalan as the mother of all chemos. It is administered by infusion for thirty minutes, just prior to the stem-cell transplant. It literally kills all cells—good and bad. It is equivalent to hitting the reboot key on a computer.

I was told to chew on ice chips the entire time the chemo was administered in order to prevent the terrible, painful mouth sores that are one of the many side effects of this particular chemo. The premedications included, among other things, Benadryl, an antihistamine that makes you sleepy. So here I was, trying to keep awake through the chemo, with a tall glass of ice chips in one hand, and grape and orange popsicles in the other. For the full hour, my focus was to stay awake and earnestly chew my ice, for fifteen minutes before the chemo, through it, and for fifteen minutes after. I was cold and fidgety but focused. But as soon as the chemo was done, I covered my head with blankets, fell asleep and snored soundly for the rest of the day. Tomorrow will be the first day of the rest of my life.

Munira, Version 2.0—Nagib

February 15, 2013

We consider February 15 to be Munira's new birthday. From a clinical perspective, this day was considered Day 0, when her stem cells were transplanted into her body. It was a terrifying and exciting venture.

The transplant process was remarkable. Two technicians in white coats arrived, pushing a rolling vault that looked like a beer keg. It contained Munira's stem cells that had been harvested back in December, which had been divided up into six individual bags for transplantation. The cells were in a flat bag, frozen and stored in a metal case that looked a little like a book. Each case was removed from the keg and checked and rechecked against the records to ensure that the stem cells were indeed Munira's. Then the case was opened and what looked like a package of frozen lean veal lay before the technician, Orlay Lopez-Perez. He removed the package and put it into a pot of water kept at 37° Celsius. To speed up the process, he even stirred the pot to help liquefy the mixture faster. A few minutes later, the warm bag of red liquid, containing mainly white blood cells and the core stem cells, was delivered to nurse Aylene under strict chain-of-custody rules. Aylene took each thawed bag, checked and rechecked it to Munira's arm band, hung it on the pole next to her and hooked it up to her Hickman line.

Being a person who loves structure and is methodical, I was fascinated by the entire process. I followed Orlay and his colleague around with a camera in hand, recording every move for posterity. Seeing how methodical and careful they were, I couldn't help but scream out loud in excitement, "THERE'S YOUR STEM CELLS BACK!" I think I shocked everyone in the room. As the first bag of stem cells was being infused into Munira, I set the camera down, and focused on my responsibility during this process, which was to keep Munira sufficiently supplied with iced popsicles.

The process of infusing all six bags took about one hour and was done within the comfort of the hospital room. It was a nice interplay of science and art, with a little bit of espionage and drama. As we expected, the transplant had Munira smelling like corn (because of the preservative used to store the stem cells), but with a touch of garlic. We were told that the smell would go away in a couple of days.

We had waited for this day for a long time, and now that it was here, we found ourselves speechless. Munira spent the entire night in prayers thanking God for not leaving her side and for making the transplant possible.

According to the physician on call that weekend, Dr Donna Reece, who heads the Molly and David Bloom Chair for Multiple Myeloma Research at the Princess Margaret, stem cells are like puzzle pieces. When transplanted, they spread around the bloodstream looking for matching receptacles to attach to. The receptacles are mainly found in the big bones of the body, such as the neck, upper and lower back, the pelvis and the upper thighs. Once attached, they start reproducing and generating new, hopefully cancer-free, cells.

Munira, as she is wont to do, started talking to her stem cells, welcoming them back to her body, asking them to make themselves at home, motivating them to attach to her bones and regenerate and produce healthy cells.

Like a phoenix rising from the ashes, Munira was reborn that day as "Munira, Version 2.0."

Stem-cell Transplant: The First Two Weeks

March 3, 2013

After that very high dose of chemotherapy on Valentine's Day and the stem-cell transplant on Day 0 (the birth of Munira, Version 2.0), the rest of the time in the hospital was a waiting game—for the stem cells to engraft and for me to manage the nasty effects of the chemo.

And what a time it turned out to be. Day one through day four were relatively easy, although Nagib had a hard time with the strong and pungent reek of creamed corn that wafted from my body for two days. I entertained visitors in the beautiful Rebecca's Hope Lounge on the 14th floor, ate Indian snacks and hot dogs, danced the hokey pokey, binge-watched Indian movies, including the beloved *Kabhi Khushi, Kabhi Gham*, and took time to rest. During those early days, my hemoglobin and platelet levels dropped and I needed blood and platelet transfusions repeatedly. But I was doing okay.

And then from day four onward, I felt like I was hit by a truck. I was so sick that I just wanted to curl up and die. All the effects of the chemo from the week before hit me with full force. And even though Dr Franke had prepared me for it, I had underestimated how sick I would get. Lifting my head from the pillow was a big deal. Taking a shower exhausted me for the rest of the day. Getting out of bed to take a walk was unimaginable. I would watch TV for a few minutes before my eyes began to close. My meal trays went untouched—I couldn't eat anything. I survived on Gatorade, ginger ale, and Ensure. All my white blood cells had been knocked down and the counts were at zero. This was expected. The stem cells were seeding and multiplying, a process that takes time and cannot be rushed. I needed to have more blood and platelet transfusions, and Neupogen injections to bring the counts up. Every day I wondered if I could do this.

And then I would take solace from my neighbor, who was a couple of days ahead of me in the process. She was going through her own challenges, which began with an allergic reaction that caused severe itching all over her body, which was now covered with angry blisters; her condition seemed to be worsening each day. We supported each other through our ups and downs and tried to maintain a semblance of normalcy and humor, including being civil about who needed to use the washroom more urgently. Unfortunately, my brave neighbor was moved to isolation and I never saw her again. I often wonder what became of her. The next day, another patient took her place in the bed beside me. She was a beautiful woman with a British accent. I would watch in amazement as she spent thirty minutes each day painstakingly applying full makeup on her porcelain skin. She had beautiful turban-style headdresses that she donned when expecting visitors. And she had many stories to tell, including one about how she met her husband and followed him from London, England to Canada.

On the night of the Oscars, I had a nose bleed, due to a low level of platelets, and it would not stop. The nurses came by frequently and asked me to put pressure on the bridge of my nose. Nagib and Shayne took turns applying the pressure; their hands became bloodied and soon there was blood on the bed. After an hour, when we thought it had stopped, the bleeding resumed, and we had to start over. Shayne was a trooper and took charge. I know he was worried; I could see it in his eyes. But he kept that to himself and showed me only love and compassion as he struggled to contain the blood. The next morning, I noticed that the shape of my nose had changed from the constant application of pressure. My face was also showing effects of water retention, and I looked like Marlon Brando in *The Godfather*—not a pretty sight.

Alia Sunderji, who is a friend of my daughter and a medical student, left me a note with a message I sorely needed right then: "Regenerating a new body full of cells can't be easy. Remember, you're allowed to be tired, fed-up, and selfish. These weeks will allow you space for that. Even mother nature feels gross and looks terrible during those gray, slushy days, in order to look radiant in the summer—as will you in the spring."

And then day 10 arrived, and things started to shift, exactly as Dr Franke had predicted. He had drawn a smiley face on the twelfth day of my calendar, telling me that it would be my Happy Day. And, miraculously, on that day, I felt that I had finally returned from the land of the living dead.

Today is two weeks from the day of the transplant and the doctors are thrilled with my recovery. They are weaning me off all antibiotics and plan to release me in the next couple of days. When I go home, I am expected to rest for three to six months and let my body heal.

As tough as the past two weeks have been, I must say that the quality of care in the stem-cell unit has been exceptional. I think it starts with Dr Franke's leadership. He believes in empowering and developing his staff. He has created a culture where nurses are comfortable making decisions and they work with a shared vision of how to look after their patients. This they do with single-minded dedication. The culture is one of competence and compassion. The nurses are like Mary Poppins. Regardless of the issue you have—diarrhea, sore throat, cough, fever, pneumonia, nosebleed, nausea, mouth sores, insomnia, dizziness— they just reach into their bags and find the right remedy. Their goal is to get you through the dark side. At one point, I was lamenting that my hair was falling out again. Voila! My nurse, Joanne, set up a makeshift barber shop in the washroom and promptly shaved my head.

During my time at the hospital, I have been able to spend dedicated time with Shayne. Some days he comes to see me for a couple of hours at night and then goes right back to work. Yesterday I threatened to hide under the covers so he would not find me. He still showed up, sat with me for a couple of hours, put me to sleep, held me close and then snuck out. I have heard from nurses in this unit that on days when I was really sick, they watched Shayne bring me food, read to me, wipe my brow, talk to me, pray for me. Most times I was oblivious to this, too sick to respond.

What price can you put on all this love, care, and compassion?

Keep on Walking

It has been one week since I came home after the stem-cell transplant. Nagib has been encouraging me to walk for fifteen minutes every day to build up my strength. The thought of leaving home was exhausting but I knew that when Nagib came back from work, he would ask me if I took that walk. Not wanting to disappoint him, I forced myself to dress up and get out of the house.

My first attempt was to take a walk around the block. Within minutes I realized that this was too ambitious; I needed to stop every few minutes to catch my breath, my heart pounding and my anxiety rising. The next day I resolved to try again and went to the small park across the street from the house—where Shayne and Sabrina used to play when they were kids. I began walking with unsteady steps around the paved edge of the playground. After a few minutes, I stopped to take refuge on a park bench. I slowly gathered some courage, caught my breath and started walking again, until I made it to the next bench less than thirty feet away. And then I began the five-minute walk back home. When I reached the house, I had barely the energy to climb up the stairs and immediately crashed into bed, my body pleading for rest.

Over the past few days, I've made my round at the park a daily ritual. I've reconnected with the East Asian umbrella-carrying couple and welcome their sunny dispositions and ready smiles. When they saw me staggering along from one bench to the next, the wife immediately offered me her arm and put an umbrella over me to shield me from the sun. The next day, both of them walked beside me, encouraging me to pick up speed. By the end of the week they had me take three rounds without a break and got me stretching as well. Each time I managed to do more, they would clap their hands and give me the thumbs-up sign—a small but meaningful recognition of my progress. I am also happy to reconnect with the spry eighty-two-year old with the toothy grin, who is a speed walker and can be seen walking the neighborhood every morning, afternoon and evening. One day I tried to join her on her walk, but after a few meters, she gave up on me and continued on her own, alone and unfettered. I've made a vow to walk along with her when I get healthy. God willing, I'll get healthy sooner rather than later.

Life After the Stem-cell Transplant

Friday marked one month since my transplant and it's not been what I had expected. I figured that once I came home, I would be able to reclaim my life with my usual vigor and energy. Instead, I take two long naps a day and then look forward to sleeping again at night. Getting a glass of water makes me tired. Eating is exhausting, so I eat in small portions.

On the plus side, my oncologist Dr Tiedemann is happy with my progress. His orders are for me to rest and let my body—and bone marrow—heal for six months. He will conduct tests in May to determine the success of the transplant. Since there is currently no cure for multiple myeloma, the stem-cell transplant, if successful, will keep the cancer at bay for a time. In Canada, this averages 2.5 years. It is expected that the cancer will come back at some point and I will require a second transplant.

In spite of these numbers, I am pretty optimistic. I plan to defy the odds. At the hospital, I met people in the ward who had not required a second transplant for five years and sometimes even longer, so I know it is possible. I also know that God is the ultimate healer and is in charge. I leave my worries with Him. Sometimes I tell Him that I would really like a cure during my lifetime. I visualize him smiling as I put my request to him somewhat repeatedly.

The biggest challenge for me right now is learning to be patient. The recovery is much slower than I would choose. The space between where I am now and where I expect to be is difficult. My emotions have been all over the place and I have been teary-eyed and sad. Part of this is due to the effects of the intense chemo that was given to me during the transplant.

Yet, slowly, things are improving and every day I am a bit stronger. I am re-learning that it is okay not to do something every day that I normally consider to be of value. I am learning that napping and sleeping are acceptable and they are the best for me right now. I am also finding it helpful to connect with individuals who've been through the transplant process, and to talk with them about shared experiences, concerns, and fears.

In the meantime, life goes on. Nagib and I are planning to go to New York in six weeks to celebrate our 31st wedding anniversary and watch the Blue Jays at the new Yankee Stadium. I am delivering a workshop on teamwork in April, my first foray back into the working world I love so much. I hope to start working out once my Hickman line is removed on March 27. And, I'm emceeing a wedding in May. These are all baby steps on the road to recovery.

Today I went to the drug store and bought a gorgeous purple eyeshadow and some beautiful lipsticks to herald the beginning of spring next week. I declare that life is to be lived—no matter what the circumstances.

Heigh-ho, Heigh-ho, It's Off to Work I Go

August 12, 2013

I'm back at work.

Throughout my battle with cancer, I kept alive the hope that I would be able to work again. I felt like I still had so much to contribute and the thought of never working again was unacceptable to me. But my reality was daunting. After the abuse that my body has taken in the past eighteen months, I was beginning to think that I would never work again.

Four months ago, I was not able to process information well at all. When someone said something to me, it would likely go over my head. I could not keep track of time, what was urgent, what was not. I often forgot. I could not concentrate on reading. This was like a death sentence. I'm a multitasker and I generally think faster than most people. Yet, while I was having chemotherapy, I found that it often took me a few days to figure out what had been said.

Shayne and Sabrina helped on this front by recording everything that my oncologist had said during my appointments, and then emailing the notes to me so I could process the information at my own pace.

"Chemo brain" is real. I started doing memory games and word searches every day to try and reverse the effects of the treatment on my brain. And slowly, very slowly, my brain started functioning again. I noticed this first when I read a paragraph in a book and did not need to reread it. I noticed this again when I stopped asking repeatedly how to do something, because I got it the first time. I could not wait to share this information with Dr Tiedemann and ask his permission to work again. He agreed that I could work one or two days a week and see how that went.

Almost immediately, I was contacted by a former client to work on a three-month project that only required a couple of days a week. I was so excited, so nervous, so anxious, so ready. To mark the occasion, Nagib dropped me off at work on the first day and took a picture of me outside the building. I felt like a little kid being taken to school on her first day.

Remember the seven dwarfs who sang: "Heigh-ho, heigh-ho, it's home from work we go?" Well, I now wake up on work days singing "Heigh-ho, heigh-ho, it's off to work I go."

I am happy to be working. It's an indescribable feeling. I feel whole and complete. My brain is back and so is my spirit. I am the same person, but a better version of myself. I've come to understand that it is impossible to go through what I have without changing at the core. I have become more loving and patient—qualities that did not come naturally to me before. Rather than jumping in with a solution, I take time to understand what is important to the person I am serving. Every moment matters. Every interaction is an opportunity to make a difference. Every day is a blessing to contribute meaningfully. I can't control what the future will bring and whether there will be a cure for my cancer. But I can sure as heck live fully in the moment.

A Milestone

August 17, 2013

Today, I reached a milestone: I combed my hair!

This is probably not earth-shattering news in the scheme of things, but for me it is huge. For almost fourteen months, I have had no hair to comb. No curls to tease. No wisps to pull. And then, over the past month, my hair follicles woke up. All of a sudden it seemed that my hair was in a race to come out after a long period of hibernation. I was curious to see its texture and color. I had heard from many cancer patients that their straight hair came back tightly curled. A couple of my cancer friends told me that they went from dark hair to a lighter shade. My hair came back straight and black. And then last week, grey made an uninvited appearance and threatened to take over the black.

I called my friend and hairdresser for advice. Afsan and I go back many years and I trust my beautiful friend, who has jet-black hair and honest opinions, to give me fashion advice. Should I go blonde? Black? Red? The conversation was pretty serious. As I have so little hair, I figured that I would pick up hair color from the pharmacy and apply it myself. Afsan told me in no uncertain terms that I was not to do that. She said that she had waited fourteen months to color my hair and I was to meet her at her salon, where she would do the honors. I came home with my newly minted hair, and my husband said he hated the color. I think all this change is hard on Nagib, since he can't figure out what the real me looks like anymore. I can sympathize, as I sometimes don't recognize myself when I happen to see my reflection in the mirror. But I have to confess that it's also kind of fun to play a little bit.

Over the past few days, I've been spending time with the little hair I have. I wash it frequently, dry it with a dryer (it takes exactly ten seconds), gel it, mousse it and run my fingers through it. I've never appreciated hair as much as I do now.

The bigger question is "what do I do with the thirteen wigs I have amassed so far?" They are wigs that allowed me to take on different personas, wigs that served me well when I needed them. I think it's time to part with them and symbolically bid adieu to cancer.

Hitting the Pause Button

During the last two years I successfully underwent treatment for lymphoma and myeloma. I return to the hospital every four months for a checkup. Life has returned pretty much to normal, the scar on my chest from the Hickman line is the only physical reminder of my battle with cancer. It has been a time of reflection and lessons learned. One of the biggest things I've learned is the importance of taking a pause. Our world demands us to be productive, fast, and efficient. Stopping and slowing down is frowned upon. There is always work to attend to, food to prepare, goals to accomplish, commitments to meet. When does one stop? Doesn't a pause for a breather interfere with all that needs to get done?

This was very much my life before I got hit with cancer. It was a life of activity, of immense productivity. I got things done. Pausing was hard for a multitasker like me. Within a five-minute time frame, I could easily be on the phone with a relative, partially listening to a documentary on TV, responding to emails, and working on my nails. Think brain traffic. I was addicted to my iPhone (the Blackberry Z10 that Nagib gifted me never stood a chance). I became an information junkie. I was convinced that Siri knew me personally. As Nagib observed me squeeze every moment of living until my eyes closed from exhaustion, he sometimes gently, sometimes more forcibly, asked me to come to bed at a reasonable hour.

But now I can no longer do that. My frayed brain no longer computes information quickly. My worn-down body limits my energy and mobility. I'm the one who holds on to the railing when climbing up and down the stairs. I am the one who looks fervently for a seat in the bus or subway as soon as I get on it. I am the one who walks slowly and sees people rush past me as if I don't exist. Sometimes I want to scream, "I wasn't always like this!" But what would that accomplish?

The world has a different texture when you move slowly. I watch blind people with seeing-eye dogs navigate through traffic. I see people using canes and walkers in grocery stores. I observe the limitations of people in wheelchairs. I witness older people in crowded places walk tentatively as if to avoid collision. And for the first time I can relate to what they are going through and feel love and compassion towards them.

By design or default, I consciously stop doing what I've been doing a couple of times a day and look around to take in what is happening around me. I pause when I don't know how to find perspective. I pause when things are not going so well in my life to see what I can learn from the experience. I pause when I am happy, just to savor the moment.

No longer does the clock govern my time; rather it is the natural rhythm of life, of listening to my body that defines how I use my time and live my life. I savor the tea I am drinking. I appreciate the crunch in my salad. I listen with full attention when someone is talking to me. I've realized that there is a heightened awareness and connection with the world and people around you when you are fully present. I just wish I could have learned this lesson an easier way.

The Footprints We Leave Behind

June 27, 2014

Perhaps they are not the stars, but rather openings in Heaven
where the love of our lost ones pours through and shines down
upon us to let us know that they are happy.

POPULAR SAYING

The thing about cancer is that you belong to a club you never wanted
to join. Membership compels you to see friends succumb to the disease
and not make it. A little bit of me dies with each loss and I pray that
God receives my friends with mercy and love. One such friend was
Pascale.

I never met Pascale face to face, yet we connected deeply. She first
wrote to me when she heard I had been diagnosed with cancer. We
worked for the same company. She was in Laval, Quebec, I was in
Toronto. She had been diagnosed with ovarian cancer, beaten it, and
returned to work. She wrote to me and asked me to be strong and to
have faith. She vowed to pray for me every day until I got better. I
believed her. And that began the story of Pascale and Munira.

Over two years, we wrote to each other often. And she would
leave comments on my blog posts—funny, thoughtful, insightful. We
became friends. One day she wrote to tell me that her cancer had come
back.

Dear Munira,

I am still reading the beautiful messages that you and your family are writing in the "I Will Survive" blog. It is always inspiring.

The day I received the one about "Setback or Speed bump" I had the news that my ovarian cancer was back and I needed to go again through chemo. It was very difficult to accept at the beginning but now we are back in good spirits . . . and seeing it as a speed bump. Of course, statistics can be depressing, but my father's prognosis was 2 to 5 years and he lived 29 years after that.

I had my first treatment on Wednesday. I do hope I will handle the side effects better. For now, as day 3 (cycle of 21 days), it is not bad at all.

This morning I was reading again this statement that your husband put in an email:

Munira's paradigm:

"I am thrilled with the care I am receiving and am confident that I will get through this. I continue to be in VERY HIGH spirits. I know that there is a master plan for why I got this and am very open to the learning, the journey, and how I can use this to make a difference in the world."

Still, I do know we are closely linked through this same experience, similar souls.

With all my affection, Pascale

In spite of going through this difficult period, Pascale kept up a wonderful, positive spirit. Whenever she had not heard from me for some time, she would write and ask how I was doing. She would share with me her personal strategies for dealing with her adversity. At one point, I teased her that I had no idea what she looked like and she sent me a picture of herself: a slender brunette in her early 50s with a kind smile, her side-swept bangs kissing her pale skin.

We continued to write to each other. With Pascale, I felt a kindred spirit, someone who could understand what I was going through. Earlier I had shared with Pascale the horrible effects of chemo and the effect of Dexamethasone on me. My dearest Pascale's words brought comfort to me and some levity to the situation. She also promised me that this was a temporary situation and that a "new and improved Munira" would emerge, with full faculties intact. I believed her.

Hello Munira,

How are you feeling?

I read your post this morning about Dexa and chemo brain and smiled all along. You know what I did a few days ago? I put the salt and pepper in the microwave . . . very bad concentration . . . my husband and I were searching everywhere to find them . . . [we found them] only because we used the microwave. We definitely need to laugh about these kinds of events. But I was not laughing after my first round of chemo, as I thought that my cognitive capacity and concentration were pretty bad. It was then that I took full consciousness that chemo was destroying bad and good cells even in my brain. I thought at the time that I will have difficulty to become as sharp as I was (and I needed to be) at the office.

My oncologist called it "deconditioning" and the great news is that all will come back. It is true. I was back to the office in March 2012 . . . I was really a better version of me. As I was focusing on the real target, I was surprised to accomplish more in a 50-hour week than spreading out my time doing the double, triple without the same results. All of this to tell you that part of your concentration is related to the fact that chemo brings a lot of fatigue and that you will get rid of it in the following months.

Anyway, Dexa and concentration are temporary situations. The real new and improved Munira will raise after the medication will be over and all your capacity will be back and even better.

Big kiss my friend. Love

Pascale

Pascale shared with me her hopes and her fears. Her family was her entire life. She spoke of the deep bond she shared with her husband, Ron, who she said was always by her side. She told me about her children, Karl and Jessica, whom she loved dearly. She spoke about her wonderful sisters. Above all, she wished to be a grandmother. I wanted this for her.

Dear Munira,

I had a beautiful Christmas time with my children Jessica and Karl. I offered them a scarf done by their mommy. I wanted them to always feel I am there surrounding them with love, keeping them in a warm embrace. I also had a great night with my sisters (I have 3 wonderful ones) and their husbands. Now I am preparing for the coming days that are always the toughest but with a better mindset than the last time and, of course, my extraordinary husband is always there by my side.

As I was wondering why me and complaining about my situation last time I wrote you, the sad event in USA with 20 young children that died just happened and overwhelmed me. How can I complain when parents who lost their children are in great pain and . . . why them? It gives me more compassion and strength to go through my own situation.

And what about you? Are you feeling good? What are the next steps for you? I am really anxious to receive more details. I pray for you every night.

Kiss and hug

With love Pascale

P.S. As I do, feel free to answer late or not if the energy is not good enough.

There were times when I was too sick to write. But Pascale continued to keep in touch with me, acutely aware of what was going on with me.

My dearest Munira,

I was reading your blog to find out that you were at the hospital beginning of the year. I hope you are back home now and feeling better.

As usual, your messages are full of important elements to meditate about life and love. It is part of the privilege to have time out of the normal crazy racing tempo and think about our priorities, what is meaningful for us, how we are meaningful for others. In the very long list of learnings, gifts and amazing people that are on our road because we are facing cancer, here you are. I feel grateful for it.

I hope this message will find you in good spirit.

Big hug

Keeping you in my prayers and love

À bientôt, Pascale

When I was preparing for my stem-cell transplant, Pascale was right there with me, encouraging and supporting me from afar. She knew when I would have my Hickman line removed and inquired about it.

In spite of her own difficulties, her compassion and love were evident with every word she wrote.

My Dear Munira,

Just a quick hello hoping that you have totally recovered from the surgery. I am excited as you are getting closer to the transplant.

Sometimes it is with mixed feeling getting closer to the end of the process as our lives have been organized around multiple medical appointments and health focus. As we are wishing so hard this is going to be over and we will get back to normal life again, it is a usual reaction to feel a little bit lost not to be surrounded by a medical team and on our own.

Anyway, I am anticipating your next step and I started to visualize beautiful, strong and healthy cells jumping and energizing your body.

Have a wonderful day. À bientôt
Pascale

Hello dear friend,

I am wondering how you are feeling both physically and spiritually. Your Hickman line was supposed to be removed 2 days ago. I hope it went well and that you are taking the best of every day.

Like you I am in the after treatment period where, most of the time, I am between sadness and high appreciation, depending on the level of fatigue.

I promise you that you will see the energy comes back slowly but surely, and you will get back to normal life . . . which is for us a beautiful target.

Kiss and hug bientôt Pascale
Just thinking of you :)

One of my favorite emails from Pascale was this one where she expressed a desire for us to meet in person. But Pascale became sicker as the cancer ravaged her body. Her emails arrived in my inbox less frequently. And each time I went to Laval for work, I asked if we could meet—but she was too weak for a visit.

Dearest Munira,

Your message was received as a gift as yesterday was a difficult day and I was far away from my regular positive thinking. I also think of you every day, wondering what are the steps you are facing, how well you are doing, what is the great thinking and spiritual mindset that keep you going.

I felt surrounded by love. I felt lucky. Most of the time, I am strong about what will come whatever it is. Yesterday, I was in the doubt. A complaining day . . . why me? What is the things I need to understand that I have not yet? Why imposing this sadness and pain to my family?

Sometimes I feel that I have crossed a door and have seen a new vision that only few people can see, using the same words that only few people can understand. Now that I know, part of me envies the rest of the people on the other side who are living like life is guaranteed for another 30 years. Part of me is so thankful now to understand I need to live fully, that life is so beautiful and that I am blessed in so many ways.

I have doubts but it is part of the journey making me a more courageous and strong person.

I received my second chemo on December 5th. Same taxol and carboplatin as it was for the first treatments and again cycle of 6 treatments every 3 weeks. Now 4 left . . . Days 3 to 6 are the toughest. Fatigue, stomach sickness, constipation . . . etc.

I manage and balance medication in a better way and try to keep busy doing some reading, painting etc. during the tough days. My husband is by my side at every minute. I am his mission.

We are preparing for a quiet Christmas knowing the third treatment is scheduled for the 26th and the New Year will be difficult to celebrate. I have lost my hair again, not a big issue, but no hair during summer time and winter time . . . what a difference!

But enough about me, how are you feeling? How is your treatment going? What are you doing these days?

Big big hug and kisses my dear Munira.

I add to my wish list to meet you in person in the coming months.

Love Pascale

A few months since I last heard from Pascale, I received a phone call from a mutual friend, Chantal, who gently told me of Pascale's passing. She told me that Pascale had been at the hospital, her health failing, her body getting weaker every day until she finally succumbed to the cancer. I was shaken to the core. I cried for hours. I felt like a part of me was destroyed. I arranged to go to Laval for the funeral. If I could not meet my friend in life, the least I could do was see her in death. Unfortunately, I was too sick to travel. Instead, I said what felt like a million prayers for Pascale on that day. Pascale believed in miracles and she was granted one when her dream of being a grandmother in her lifetime was fulfilled. I like to believe that when we lose someone we love, they continue to be with us in memories and in words. Pascale will live on in her husband, her children and in her granddaughter Rachel. She left behind a legacy of compassion, of love, of spirit, of positive energy, of strength and grace and especially of joy.

Kwaheri Canada, Karibu Kenya—Shayne

August 31, 2014

It has been just over two and a half years since my mom's cancer diagnosis and eighteen months since a stem-cell transplant gave her a new lease on life. My mom's journey has had a profound effect on me. After six years of investment banking, I left my job. Spending seventy-plus hours at work every week didn't seem to make much sense anymore. I grew up a child of immigrant parents, believing that you must work extraordinarily hard and make sacrifices in your twenties and thirties to build a successful life and secure your future. But now, life feels too short.

Shortly after resigning, I took an unpaid consulting position with a not-for-profit organization in Cairo, Egypt. I joked with former colleagues that I needed to "cleanse my soul" after too many years surrounded by money. In reality, I always wanted to see the world and make an impact, like Sabrina has been doing in East Africa, but I was too busy focusing on my career to follow through on this. But now it was time to follow that dream.

My mom's battle with cancer also took a toll on my long-time relationship. My girlfriend and I broke up a few months ago. We grew apart over the last two years, as I wasn't always able to communicate the dizzying array of emotions I was experiencing, finding myself unable to focus on much beyond work and family. I distinctly remember a friend of hers commenting, "Shayne just has this aura of sadness around him these days." I knew her friend was right.

But like the silver lining that my mom discovered through her journey with cancer, I feel that this situation has given me a new lease on life. After finishing my assignment in Cairo, I made a spontaneous trip to Nairobi, Kenya to visit Sabrina. I always regretted not visiting East Africa (the "motherland") with the rest of my family a few years ago, a time when I couldn't fathom requesting a two-week holiday from work. After a mechanical issue with the plane, a few flight delays and ten hours of waiting at Cairo International Airport, I finally arrived in Nairobi. My sister's regular driver, Eugene, was waiting with a name card in hand. He spoke perfect English and carried an iPad with two different navigational apps in his car.

"How can a Kenyan taxi driver have an iPad?" I thought, clinging to an outdated stereotype. As we drove into the city, I witnessed hordes of men emerging from the informal settlements, dressed in freshly-pressed suits, colorful ties, and newly polished loafers that would impress even the most discerning of my former investment banker colleagues. "How can people in slums afford suits and how do they keep their shoes so shiny." In this moment, I remembered one of my mom's favorite quotes: labels are for jars, not people.

Tomorrow is actually my first day of work. During my visit to Nairobi, I landed a contract with the International Finance Corporation, the investment arm of the World Bank Group. I went back and forth on whether to accept the contract. On the one hand, I wanted to return to Toronto for a few months and spend dedicated time with my family. If my mom's cancer experience taught me anything, it was that I needed to prioritize what is most important to me. On the other hand, this contract is an incredible opportunity to pivot my life to a completely different direction. At first, I felt selfish making my decision, but when I asked my parents for their opinion, they were united in their response: "We don't want you to put your life on hold any longer. Take the job. No question."

Kwaheri Canada. Karibu Kenya.

The New Normal

November 2015

I saw myself as a cancer survivor, having cheated death twice in the past two years. But I wanted to do more than just survive. I wanted to thrive. I wanted to get back to feeling the way I did before. I wanted to live well. I wanted to function on five hours of sleep again. I wanted to reclaim my life and make up for lost time.

Befitting my Type A personality, I set lofty goals for myself. I was going to start work immediately. I was going to lead volunteer projects as a way to give back. I was going to exercise every day, maybe twice a day. The list was never-ending and ambitious.

Very rapidly, I realized that my body was not ready and I simply did not have the energy to do what my mind desired. The chemo had taken its toll. My stamina was nowhere close to where it was pre-cancer. My hair came back patchy and I could see bald spots. A couple of my teeth fell out. There were days when I would cry myself to sleep, feeling inadequate and hopeless. After many such nights, I realized that I needed a new strategy. Rather than ambitious, out-of-the-park home runs, I needed to enjoy accomplishing small things: reading one chapter instead of an entire book in one sitting, cleaning a drawer instead of attacking the entire home, climbing a flight of stairs without getting out of breath. I started to give myself more time than usual for ordinary events: two hours to get ready to go to jamatkhana, rather than my customary fifteen minutes. I had to learn that my emotions were all over the place and the smallest thing could lead to a massive outburst. One of the hardest parts was recognizing that I could not go back to work full time, since I did not have the stamina to manage an eight-hour work day.

The good news was that every day my body was healing, and as I felt stronger, I was able to accomplish more. Taking a bath would not exhaust me, going out for a coffee with a friend was manageable. I put all my energies into moving forward. Slowly, I found my new normal. And this new normal lasted three months, until there was an even better new normal, and then another.

About six months post-transplant, I started to function almost like my pre-cancer normal. My head sported hair. I needed less sleep. I could manage a full day of shopping. I took on a long-term consulting assignment, and Nagib and I became more active with the Toronto & District Multiple Myeloma Support Group. Life became comfortable and I happily jumped into my various roles—as mom, wife, friend, daughter, and colleague. These were some of my happiest days.

Some of my toughest days over the cancer diagnoses was when I saw death come knocking on a number of my friends' doors. There was Nazim Hirani, a community leader from our jamatkhana, whom I have known for more than thirty years, who passed away from lymphoma. Shah Ramji, from my hometown in Moshi, whom I knew my entire life, was also claimed by cancer. I went to their funerals and mourned the loss of wonderful individuals whose lives had been taken too quickly. Closer to home, my cousin in Edmonton, Alnasir Dadani, lost his life to multiple myeloma and I witnessed how devastating his loss was for his mom, wife, children, brother, and sister and indeed the whole family. My mom, who saw Alnasir like her own son, went to his funeral and every day for two months after she returned home, I saw her wipe away tears as she remembered him.

Tony Gemmiti's loss affected me profoundly. I vividly remember the first time I met Tony and his wife Mary when, on a cold February afternoon in 2014, the couple entered the Myeloma Support Group meeting, fresh snowflakes on their coats. Tony had been diagnosed with myeloma in October 2012 and had his stem-cell transplant in

December 2013. As the meeting progressed, I watched Tony and Mary in admiration. It was hard not to notice them. They were playful and often stealing glances at each other. They had an easy comfort about them that comes from being together for thirty years. They appeared to have a rich life and a great marriage. He proclaimed that she was the best caregiver possible. We hit it off with the Gemmitis immediately and they included us in their world. Alas, Tony's myeloma came back and his second stem-cell transplant in March 2014 did not take. He was put on a clinical trial and the Gemmiti family were optimistic that a miracle would occur. I was delighted to see Tony and his extended family at the Princess Margaret Journey to Conquer Cancer on June 22, 2014. Although he was a shadow of himself and had lost a lot of weight, he had that mischievous smile, and the bright eyes still sparkled. At the Walk he said to me, "Munira, you and I are on a parallel journey. We are going to fight this together."

Four days after the walk, Mary, Tony's wife, wrote to me to say that Tony was taken off the clinical trial and was being put in palliative care. She said that we could come and see him at the hospital. I cried as I heard this news. I did not feel strong enough to see Tony right away and told her that I would come by and visit him when I was next at the hospital the following week. I never saw Tony again. He passed away on July 3, 2014, at the age of 53. Nagib, Sabrina, and I went to Tony's visitation. If the wealth of a person is counted by the people who love them, then Tony Gemmiti was a rich man. The visitation was a reminder to me of this world that I am now a part of. For the first time since my diagnosis, I wondered how long I had to live and the impact my death would have on my family. Mary told me that while Tony knew that he could not be saved from his devastating illness, he was optimistic that the funds raised for the Journey to Conquer Cancer would help other patients. To keep Tony's dream alive, I will continue to fight and battle the cancer, and keep Tony's memory in my heart every day.

During the two-year remission following my recovery, some devastating news hit even closer to home. My sister was diagnosed with uterine cancer and underwent surgery and radiation. She was a trooper and embraced her treatment with ease and grace. Nagib was diagnosed with early stage prostate cancer, too young to fall prey to this. He was seen at the Princess Margaret Cancer Centre and St Michael's Hospital. It was surreal for us to go to Princess Margaret for Nagib's doctors' appointments and walk the familiar corridors on the fourth floor, where the chemo center was located. We were both shaken as our memories came flooding back, now with our roles reversed: he the patient, I his caregiver. Nagib's approach to his cancer was to do his homework and arm himself with information. He consulted everything he could—data, studies, numbers, videos, research papers, medical journals—to make sense of the cancer. And he approached this information objectively, looking for patterns and creating educated guesses and hypotheses. But he preferred to do this alone, with no desire to share his feelings with me. This irked me, since I wanted to talk about everything—what he was thinking, how he was feeling, his fears. As a caregiver, I had to learn how to meet Nagib where he was at, so I could find clues about how to give him support when he needed it. It really did give me first-hand experience of what Nagib had to go through as my caregiver—feeling helpless and anxious and sometimes woefully inadequate. Nagib's prostate cancer was determined to be early stage (Stage I) and, after a minor procedure, he was put on an active surveillance program during which his PSA (Prostate-Specific Antigen) score was monitored carefully. Thankfully, the PSA scores have remained stable.

We have endured a lot over the past five years and have somehow found a way through it, stronger and better. I needed to draw on this strength recently, when a few days ago during a routine doctor's appointment, I received blood results that showed that I was at severe risk of contracting an auto-immune disease. An auto-immune disease is when your immune system attacks healthy cells. It can affect any number of organs. I have been immunocompromised by my bout with cancer, but these new results showed that the condition could become severe. My family doctor was surprised that I was not showing any symptoms, so the plan has been to wait and watch. While I was contemplating what to do with this new condition, I noticed a lump in my right breast.

4.

BREAST CANCER

Breast Cancer at a Glance

What Is Breast Cancer?

Breast cancer starts in the cells of the breast. Normally, healthy breast cells grow, divide, and die in an orderly way. Cancer cells multiply in an uncontrolled fashion and create a lump or tumor, or damage healthy tissue.

There are many types of breast cancer. Some of the more common include:

Ductal carcinoma in situ. "In situ" is good; it means that the cancer is contained within the milk ducts and has not spread.

Invasive ductal breast cancer. "Invasive" is not good. Here the cancer cells have spread from the milk ducts to the surrounding breast tissue. This is the most common type of breast cancer.

Breast Cancer Statistics

The prognosis for breast cancer depends on many things, including a patient's health history, the size of the tumor, the stage of the cancer, and whether it has spread to the lymph nodes. According to the Canadian Cancer Society, it is estimated that in 2019, 27,200 women will be diagnosed with breast cancer and 5,100 women will die from it. The five-year survivor rate for breast cancer is 88 percent (the ten-year survivor rate is 82 percent).

Symptoms

Breast cancer is typically diagnosed by self-examination, a clinical exam by a doctor, a mammogram, an ultrasound, or a biopsy. According to the Canadian Cancer Society, the most common early symptom of cancer is a hard lump in the breast. Other symptoms can include the hardening of the tissue in the breast, a lump in the armpits, changes in the shape or size of the breast or nipple, and discharge from the nipple.

Treatment

The most common treatments for breast cancer are surgery, radiation therapy, chemotherapy, hormonal therapy, and biological therapy.

Source:
   https://www.cancer.ca

Here We Go Again

December 2, 2015

It began in November 2015, when I found a tiny lump in my right breast. I casually mentioned it to Nagib, and his reaction was, "I don't want to hear about it." We laughed it off, thinking there was no way it could be anything, and went on with our day. The next day I checked again and felt an unmistakable, miniscule lump. I went to my family doctor, Dr Hovsep Baghdadlian, a chatty, amiable man who uses his training as an internal medicine specialist to provide the best care to his patients. He tried to locate the lump but could not find it. Could it be my imagination? He trusted me enough to arrange a mammogram for me. The first mammogram was inconclusive, so he sent me for a second one. A tiny speck was found, and he gave me an urgent referral for a biopsy and ultrasound at the North York General Hospital. I was hopeful that the results would come out negative and there was nothing to worry about. "Much ado about nothing," I said to myself.

On December 2, 2015, Nagib and I met Dr Brian Pinchuk, an oncological surgeon at North York General's Breast Centre. He told us that the results of the biopsy showed that I had invasive ductal carcinoma. That tiny, barely detectable lump was the sign of a cancer that had spread into two lymph nodes under my right arm. I was too shocked to know how to respond. One cancer was bad enough. Two cancers were hard to accept. Three cancers were just a cruel joke. Do I cry? Do I say this can't be happening? Do I give up on life?

We called Dr Tiedemann, my oncologist at Princess Margaret, to ask if it was normal for someone with my history to get breast cancer. He said that it was highly unusual and that perhaps I was "just unlucky." He recommended that I undergo genetic sequencing to determine whether there was a specific gene in my body that was the culprit, making me more susceptible to cancer. This of course had me worried that Shayne and Sabrina might also be susceptible.

The hardest part was the impact this news had on my family. Nagib looked shell-shocked. Shayne was in Kenya. When he heard the news, the first thing he said was, "I am so glad to be coming home in two weeks." Sabrina, who was doing her Masters degree in Development Practice at Columbia University in New York, was in between classes and could only talk for a few minutes. She thanked us for not keeping the news from her. My mom fought back tears.

The sadness within the family was palpable. It felt as though a deep cloud had enveloped us; none of us knew how to lift it. I felt guilty about putting my family through another ordeal and wondered if my battle was worth fighting anymore. How much more could they handle? This was the closest to a breaking point that I had felt in a long time.

I dealt with this new diagnosis by learning as much as I could about breast cancer. I was curious about God's plan for me. Was it that I should learn about another type of cancer so I could extend my reach and support more people?

The next steps now were additional tests, including a complete CT scan and a bone scan to determine the stage of the cancer and the treatment plan. As Nagib aptly put it: "Here we go again."

Breast Cancer 101

December 13, 2015

It's been a tough couple of weeks since I was diagnosed with breast cancer. In that time, I have vacillated from being totally zombielike to wanting to take control of this new beast. I wonder if this cancer will have an impact on my previous cancers. I am confused about the treatment options. My state of mind is dismal, at best, and the slightest provocation causes me to burst into tears. I know that our best defense is to learn as much as we can about this cancer so that we can be active participants and advocates when we meet with the medical team at North York General Hospital in a couple of weeks to discuss the treatment plan. We opted for North York General because it has a state-of-the-art breast cancer center; Dr Tiedemann is comfortable that I will receive quality care there. Also, it is only ten minutes away from home.

My treatment will depend on the type of breast cancer I have, including the stage and grade. The treatment also depends on the hormone receptor status, in other words, whether the cancer cells have receptors for the hormones estrogen and progesterone. My biopsy results came back estrogen positive, meaning that the tumor was much more likely to respond to hormone therapy. I was also tested for human epidermal growth factor receptor 2 (HER-2), which controls how a healthy breast cell grows, divides, and repairs itself. My biopsy showed that I am HER-2 positive, which is more aggressive than other breast tumors, and indicates that the cells are dividing and growing uncontrollably.

This week, I had two additional tests: a full-body scan and a bone scan. I am hoping that these tests will show that my cancer has not spread beyond one or two lymph nodes in my underarm. If it has, I am in deep trouble. The plan is for me to meet the oncologist who has been assigned to my case, Dr Danny Robson, next Friday to get the test results and finalize a treatment plan. Unfortunately, based on preliminary discussions, it appears that this will include chemo, surgery and radiation.

In the meantime, I will be injected with markers (titanium clips) in my breast and in the affected lymph nodes. If the chemo works so well that the doctors can no longer find the cancer, the markers will show them where the tumor was.

The medical team has "strongly recommended" that I see a psychiatrist who specializes in oncology. I don't know if they do this for all their breast cancer patients, or figure that I need one because, as Dr Pinchuk says, I am a "complex case" who is going through "more stuff than any person should go through." I am keeping an open mind and will go to at least the first appointment, which is scheduled for January.

Playing the Hand You Have Been Dealt

December 24, 2015

Complex. Complicated. Unique. Every doctor I have seen has uttered these words several times while reviewing my case with me. Three cancers in three and a half years is rare, more so when there is no history of cancer in the immediate family.

A week after the tests, Nagib, Shayne, Sabrina and I met with Dr Robson to discuss my results. We clung to his every word. For any cancer patient, the worst word in the English language is "metastasis." It means that the cancer has spread from its initial site to another part of the body, making it difficult to treat, because now several organs are involved. We were hoping that this was not the case for me. It would have been too much to bear.

Dr Robson summarized the test results. The bone scan showed regular degeneration consistent with my recent battle with multiple myeloma (which we expected). The CT scan showed that the new cancer had not spread to any other part of the body, beyond the one or two lymph nodes in my right underarm. We gave a collective sigh of relief.

Dr Robson then proposed a treatment plan. If I were not complex, complicated, and unique, as he described me, the plan would be to have four months of chemotherapy, then a break for a month, followed by surgery to remove the lump and some lymph nodes, followed further by radiation—a "typical" approach for a diagnosis of early-stage breast cancer. He expressed concern, however, that the chemotherapy would wear down my bone marrow and compromise my ability to deal with the multiple myeloma by jeopardizing the second stem-cell transplant that I would eventually need.

Therefore, he said, I should have the surgery first, and then, based on the outcome, the medical team would determine the need, benefits, and downstream implications of additional treatments, such as hormone therapy, radiation and, if necessary, chemotherapy. Dr Tiedemann, with the support of the breast cancer team at Princess Margaret, was weighing in on the decision-making, which gave me a lot of comfort. We hoped to confirm the plan and begin prepping for treatment at the end of December.

As I discussed the situation with my family the next morning, Sabrina compared my condition over the past few years to the weather system: most days have been delightfully sunny, others, cloudy with scattered showers. And even when we were battling thundershowers, the sun always found a way to peek through and clear the rain. My latest diagnosis means a rainstorm is in the forecast. Rather than fighting it or complaining about it, I decided that we were all going to put on our rain boots, get out our umbrellas and face the storm head on. Knowing us, we'll probably splash into a few puddles and sing in the rain along the way! Because, we know, the sun will come again soon. It always does.

The Plan

December 29, 2015

Someone asked me yesterday how I do it. How do I manage to keep it all together in the face of this brand-new breast cancer diagnosis? Isn't it too much? The truth is, sometimes I function somewhat normally, other times I feel like I am being pulled into a dark vortex with no way out. I have been through two cancers so I'm no longer crippled by fear. Yet, I felt—if I remember rightly—the same sense of anxiety and foreboding as I did with my previous cancers as I waited for my appointment with Dr Pinchuk, the surgeon at North York General Hospital who would remove the tumor from my breast.

Dr Pinchuk was a young, good-natured, well-dressed man with a wonderful smile. He went through my diagnosis and potential treatment with clarity and precision. He was efficient but did not rush. When we had questions, he answered them simply, in layman terms. I loved how he drew pictures, carefully labeled and drawn to scale, to explain what he was going to do to remove the tumor. For a doctor, he had excellent handwriting! When you're thrust into the health care system, it's easy to feel like an insignificant widget in a long assembly line. Dr Pinchuk had a way of making us feel comfortable.

I left the appointment with a plan and a clear sense of direction. My biggest takeaway was that breast cancer has fairly straightforward treatment options, depending on the type of cancer you have.

If you have invasive ductal carcinoma, are estrogen positive, and HER-2 positive (as I am), then the treatment generally calls for chemo, surgery, radiation, and hormone therapy. If you are neither estrogen nor HER-2 positive, then the treatment is typically just a lumpectomy (removal of the lump). If you are estrogen positive, but not HER-2 positive, then there is a different, "standard" treatment procedure.

In a strange way, there is comfort in knowing that breast cancer research has advanced to a stage where there is almost a cookie-cutter approach to how it is treated. This is in stark contrast to what I experienced with lymphoma and myeloma, where the treatment was more like a complicated spider chart, with all kinds of equations and computations.

Unfortunately, my case is anything but usual, so the standard course of treatment does not apply. We all chuckled when Dr Pinchuk said that Dr Robson had used the word *unique* at least ten times in his report to describe my history and his recommendation for a treatment specific to my situation (in consultation with Princess Margaret).

The plan is for me to have surgery on January 26, 2016 (a lumpectomy as well as the removal of all the lymph nodes from my right armpit). This will be followed, a month later, by radiation, five days a week for five weeks. If all goes according to plan, the surgery and radiation will be completed by April. This means I can look forward to going to Sabrina's graduation in New York and be back to full strength before her wedding in July.

That night, as I was describing the plan to my mom, she held my hands and said, "You can't die before I do." I told her that I would have a word with God. I love my mom with all my heart and understood what she left unsaid. A parent should never have to bury their child; it is not part of life's natural order and rhythm.

As difficult as these cancers have been on me, the effects are written all over my bald head, my fluctuating weight, my bruised arms. I receive endless support because of these observable symbols. Sometimes I think it's harder for my family, whose battle wounds lie below the surface. Their outward strength masks the pain they go through. It's in the small comments like my mom's that I realize it has not been easy for them. At times I feel helpless but then I ask myself,

"What's in my control?" I can't control the treatment schedule or the side effects. I can't control the outcome. But I can remain positive, I can make an effort to get out of bed in the morning, I can look at each new day as a re-start. And when I do, I realize that my family takes their cue from me and they worry just a little bit less.

A Textbook Surgery

The procedure I had was the removal of the radioactive seed localization in my right breast, which had been placed previously as a locator of the cancerous lump; this was followed by a lumpectomy, or removal of the lump, and finally a complete removal of the neighboring lymph nodes.

As I lay waiting outside the surgical room on a gurney, Amin Naran, a friend who worked at the hospital, came by. He said he saw my name on the roster and had been expecting me, and had a gift tucked away for me. He left and quickly returned with a pillow (apparently, they are in short supply) and expertly positioned it under my head so I could rest comfortably. He then told the OR staff to take extra special care of me because I was his friend. God sends angels in many ways.

The mood in the operating room was relaxed. Everyone there took time to introduce themselves and to ask how I was doing. There was a humanity that was refreshing. As the anesthesiologist searched for a cooperative vein, Dr Pinchuk held my hand the entire time. I asked him about his plans for the rest of the day and he said he was excited to take his kid swimming after work. It's hard to imagine doctors who deal with the vicissitudes of life and death having normal lives. He left to "get his headlights" to start the surgery. His assistant, with a big smile and bright yellow personality, took his place beside me. This simple gesture—not being left alone at a vulnerable time   left me teary eyed.

This was the first time I ever had surgery. To prepare, Nagib read everything he could about the procedure, logically processed every fact, and shared key information with me. I, on the other hand, approached the surgery in large strokes (right breast, remove tumor and lymph nodes) underpinned by hope and faith that everything would turn out well.

While I was in the operating room, Nagib spent the day pacing, from the crowded waiting room to the somewhat quieter cafeteria downstairs (where he comforted himself with coffee). Every so often, he would rush back upstairs to the waiting room to check the scoreboard and update the results on WhatsApp to Shayne in Nairobi and Sabrina in New York. Two hours later, I emerged from the operating room, and a well-caffeinated Nagib was relieved to hear that the surgery had gone according to plan.

More Bad News

February 10, 2016

Devastated. Hopeless. Unsettled.

That is how I felt after my post-operative follow-up appointment with Drs Pinchuk and Robson.

I had gone to the appointments full of optimism, expecting to hear that my breast cancer was mostly gone and receive dates to start radiation treatment, after which I would be completely in the clear. But that's not what happened.

Dr Pinchuk started by saying that my surgery was successful. He had removed the tiny 14 mm tumor, as well as surrounding tissue. The pathology report showed that there was no remaining cancer in my breast. He checked the site of the surgery and told me that I was healing as expected. But even as he was giving me this great news, I felt uneasy. I felt in my gut that there was more information coming—and it would not be good news. I was right.

Dr Pinchuk had removed 16 lymph nodes from my underarm. The pathology report showed that every one of them had cancer:

Lymph Nodes
    Sentinel and Non-Sentinel Nodes
        Total Number of Lymph Nodes Examined: 16
        Micro/Macro Metastases: Present
        Number of Lymph Nodes with Macrometastases: 15

Number of Lymph Nodes with Micrometastases: 1
Size of Largest Metastatic Deposit: 35 mm
Extranodal Extension: Present

Metastases—how I hate that word! It says that the cancer has spread from its original tumor site. How did I not feel a lump bigger than 1.5 inches under my arm?

This was devastating news. Based on the observations, my diagnosis was confirmed as Grade 2 DCIS (ductal invasive carcinoma in situ), estrogen positive, progesterone negative, HER-2 positive, with metastases in the lymph nodes. In other words, Stage 3 advanced breast cancer.

Dr Robson indicated that it was highly likely that my breast cancer would return—and return with a vengeance—if it was not treated aggressively. There was no choice but to go for chemotherapy, even if it compromised a second stem-cell transplant in the future when my myeloma would inevitably return.

So the plan is for six cycles of chemotherapy to be given intravenously every three weeks for 18 weeks, beginning mid-March, after I have healed from the recent surgery. This will take me to mid-June and give me enough time to recover before Sabrina's wedding at the end of July. After the chemo, I will need targeted radiation treatment to zap any cancer cells that still remain. The radiation is expected to take five weeks, every day from Monday to Friday. And then there is antibody therapy, anti-hormone pills and, sometime down the road, bone-strengthening therapy.

I am not sure how to process this information and am sitting at a place of loss, of sadness, of trying to make sense of this. Yesterday I was sobbing so much that poor Dr Pinchuk kept coming back to ask if there was anything he could do. He gave me a bottle of water. Then he gave me a power bar—and one for Nagib. I continue to shed many tears today as I think of what lies ahead.

The PICC Experience Again

Patients who go through cancer treatment do not generally require a PICC line; they get chemotherapy through a temporary IV inserted into a vein in their arm. But we had found during my past cancer treatments at Princess Margaret that I have nonfunctioning veins in my arms and inserting an IV was almost impossible.

So, today was an eventful day. I went with Nagib, ready and optimistic, to have a PICC line inserted into a vein above the bend of my elbow on the inside part of my left arm. Unfortunately, the procedure turned out to be anything but simple. My doctors had a difficult time finding a vein (using an ultrasound) in which to place the PICC catheter. My veins chose to play a wicked game of hide-and-seek, while my arteries were feeling playful and kept rising to the top and hiding the veins. I apologized to the doctors for making their work so hard, and they kept reiterating that I should not apologize because—you guessed it—I was special. And as I lay on the cold surgical bed, I kept thinking, "For once, I wish I was ordinary."

The doctors called in a senior technician, who poked around and found a good vein on his second try. Just to be sure, they X-rayed my arm to check that everything was in place. A huge relief. The doctor who did this procedure spent five minutes giving me a pep talk about being positive, having faith, and building my immunity.

Now the challenge is to keep the PICC line clean and dry, which will make taking a shower every day difficult. Swimming, a new activity that's been added to my repertoire this past year, is off-limits. I will also need to get the site cleaned at a local clinic on a weekly basis to prevent infection.

Chemotherapy starts tomorrow. In anticipation of not being able to enjoy food for the next few months, I decided to go on an eating binge. Nagib took me to one of my favorite haunts, Szechuan Gourmet, for lunch, where we ate ginger chicken and peanut chicken. For dinner, my mom made chicken curry, roti, and rice. And then I gobbled up two KitKat chocolate bars, probably not what I should have eaten, but my body was craving food—and lots of it.

The best part of today was picking up Sabrina from the airport. She has spring break and has come home from New York to be with me for my first chemo. I am just beaming from ear-to-ear because we will spend the next ten days with her. She makes everything better.

Please—Sabrina

I'm on a flight home from New York for spring break. While many of my friends will be gallivanting around East Timor and Peru this week, there's only one place I want to be: home.

When my mom was first diagnosed with two cancers in 2012, I was working in Kenya at a large nonprofit organization. What had started as a short-term fellowship turned into a full-time job, managing maternal and child health projects across the region. I loved my work and though my circumstances were diametrically opposite to everything I was familiar with in Canada, I felt a sense of belonging in East Africa. I lived in the same apartment complex as my great-grandmother had, went on dates to the same places my mom had frequented as a teenager, and connected with family that I hadn't known I had. But when I got the call informing me about my mom's cancers, there was no need to think: I knew I had to be there by her side.

I spent ten months in Toronto tag-teaming with my dad to share caregiving responsibilities. The hospital became our second home. There was a physical and mental exhaustion that accompanied every treatment, every doctor's appointment, every night spent in the emergency room.

When my mom went into remission, my identity as a caregiver collapsed—she no longer needed me to help her with basic tasks. I realized that it was time to refocus on my life. I was twenty-five years old and my world had been opened up to the possibilities of doing meaningful work in East Africa. And yet, I also understood the unpredictability of life and had a strong desire to spend time with my family.

I decided to go to graduate school in the US, making frequent trips back to Kenya to pursue an idea for an early childhood social enterprise that was beginning to take shape. During this time, my dad was diagnosed with early stage prostate cancer and my aunt underwent treatment for uterine cancer. And just when we thought we couldn't handle anything more, my mom has been diagnosed with an aggressive breast cancer.

On the flight, I open up my journal and write:

Dear God,

I hate it. Why her? Why again? It's not fair. She's been through so much already. More than any one person should stand in a lifetime. Please take care of her this time around. As she starts her new round of chemo, please be with her; every step of the way. The way her kidney stone passed without any pain all those years ago—that's the type of looking after we need from you again. You can do it. I know you can. You can do anything. She doesn't need to suffer any longer. Let's just give her some chemo, give her some radiation and then have the cancer be all gone away. And don't let the myeloma come back either. Let it miraculously disappear so she can live a long, healthy life with the love of her life. I'm worried about Daddy—I don't think he could survive if anything happened to her. If you need to take her, make sure she comes all the way to you—no passing go, no collecting $200; just a straight line up to you so she doesn't need to go through any more tests. She's passed all the tests. Or at least, give me her tests. I'll pass them for her. Just don't let her suffer anymore—please. Please. What can I give you in return? I'll do anything. Just no more cancers, no more sickness. A long, insanely happy & healthy life—that's all I ask for her.

Please.

Thank you. Sorry, I forgot to say thank you in advance.

Back on the Chemo Train

March 11, 2016

Today, I started chemo treatment for breast cancer. I've had chemo before, so this feels like a familiar experience, though it's also different. It's like taking the same journey but to a different place.

North York General Hospital does a fantastic job of preparing patients for chemotherapy. Every chemotherapy patient attends a comprehensive orientation class before treatment starts. At this class, held every Friday, we heard from a pharmacist, who gave us a time line of what to expect during a three-week chemo cycle: nausea for the first five days, mouth sores around day 10, expected hair loss between days 15 and 25 and fatigue the entire time. A dietician talked about the best foods to eat while undergoing chemo. This was followed by a social worker, who talked about the kind of support the hospital could provide (counseling for self and family, financial assistance, transportation). The session concluded with instructions from a nurse on the blood-work regimen, the length of the chemo treatment (generally four to eight hours), and a tour of the chemo clinic.

My first day of chemo for breast cancer was scary. I ended up with an allergic reaction to one of the chemo drugs—Taxotere—that caused me to have sudden severe back spasms, neck pain, and difficulty in breathing. I was extremely scared and wondered if I was going to die. The nurses calmly gathered around me and immediately stopped the chemo treatment. Then they proceeded to give me an antidote that controlled the side effects. I needed oxygen after the bad reaction and the head nurse slid the picture frame behind me on the wall to reveal emergency equipment hidden behind the soothing picture of a blue sky and the sea. They put an oxygen mask on me and once everything was under control, and with Dr Robson's approval, they administered Taxotere again, much slower this time to avoid the reaction. While they administered the chemo drugs, I had to keep my fingers and toes in ice packs so that my fingernails and toenails would not be harmed by the harsh drugs.

Going through chemo brings you head to head with the cost of pharmaceuticals. Typically for patients in Ontario, the cost of the in-hospital drugs are covered, while drugs required out of hospital are not covered. You have to rely on the compassion of the pharmaceutical manufacturer to give you the medication for free or your group insurance plan (if you have one) and that, too, has annual maximums that you will likely blow through very quickly. For instance, I need to be injected with Neulasta after each chemo treatment to increase the white cells in my body. Neulasta costs approximately $3,000 per needle and I need six of these injections for the six cycles of chemo, totaling $18,000, well above the maximum annual limit of our group insurance plan.

To mitigate the financial burden on my family, we must work with our insurance company to gain access to the Victory Program (funded by the drug company Amgen that makes Neulasta), as well as the Government of Ontario's Trillium Drug Program (which is income-tested) to figure out how best to get the medications I need without being too much out-of-pocket. This is a time-consuming process that requires phone calls with all the stakeholders, including the medical reimbursement team at the hospital, the pharmacy, and government agencies. It also requires the completion of forms requiring extensive details. Unfortunately, with all the assistance available, we still find ourselves out-of-pocket every time I need a major intervention. I do not see this situation changing anytime soon, since I will continue to need costly medication from time to time as my cancer progresses. This has caused us financial strain, particularly as my income has reduced by 80% in the past few years. Still, I am exceedingly thankful that we live in Canada, where resources and treatments are available, and most medications are paid for by the government. I often wonder how individuals with major illnesses manage in countries where universal health care is not available.

As I leave the hospital today, the drugs pumping through my body, I reflect: one chemo down, only five more to go!

"Oh Yeah, I Remember That"

March 29, 2016

It has been two weeks since my first chemotherapy treatment, and everything is coming back to me like an old, familiar song. The first week after chemo was tough. Nausea and frequent trips to the bathroom. Never-ending nosebleeds and painful mouth sores. Everything tasting like sawdust. The fatigue that saw me sleeping for fourteen hours a day. And the chemo-brain syndrome that reduced my ability to think and caused me to forget simple things. It's the forgetting of things that dismays me the most. Simple routine tasks that I've done effortlessly a million times are proving to be complicated. I find myself standing in front of the fridge uncertain of what I was looking for or staring at the compost, garbage, and recycle containers, trying to figure out what goes where. One day I took Nagib's prized leather briefcase to get the zipper fixed. When it came time to pick up the briefcase, I could not remember which store I had taken it to. I went to one store, and then another, and then a third, until I found the right store and recovered the bag. This reduced me to tears and caused me to have a meltdown for a few hours. And then, just like that, everything changed a week later. I started to taste food again and I have rediscovered my love affair with oranges and Cadbury Whole Nut chocolate bars. The fatigue has lifted and I have tons of energy.

So how am I managing this rollercoaster? I think it has helped that I have gone through chemo twice before, so I know what to expect and trust that I will come out the other side of it. As I go through the different side effects, I find myself saying, "Oh yeah, I remember that!" and then promptly find a way to deal with it. The familiar habits that help me ride through the chemo are coming back. Carrot juice and beets every day. Green smoothies. Vitamins. Ensure nutritional shakes for when I can't eat. Sleep when I need it. Walks to keep my body moving. And getting things done when I have short bursts of energy. Chemo, with all its side effects, feels much more manageable when you stop fighting it and listen to your body.

Today, my hair has started to fall out. This is something I was expecting and it is not as devastating as it was when it happened four years ago. I am holding on to my hair, literally, for as long as I can before I start sporting wigs. My friend and hairstylist Afsan took Sabrina and me wig-shopping last week. Although I have thirteen old wigs from my previous cancers, I decided that it was time to donate those and start afresh.

My past collided with my present as the owners of the wig place remembered me from four years ago and helped me find the newest styles and colors. They wanted me to go a bit wild and showed me wigs with updos and exotic styles and colors. It was one of my tired days and I did not feel like playing, so I opted for four wigs that I could see myself wearing every day.

I hung on to my hair until bald patches started appearing scattered across my head. Afsan came to the rescue and shaved my head, while Nagib looked on nervously.

The next day my friend Tarquin Singh came home and applied a stunning henna crown on my head. Tarquin operates a company called Henna Planet. She designs crowns after consulting with the client, so it is a wonderful process of co-creativity. I told her to find a way to include the words "when you choose hope" at the back of the crown and she did.

I cherish the experience of working with Tarquin. While she applied the henna, we talked about life and work and children. Every once in a while, she had to remind me to be still so she could trace the intricate design on my head. I am always stunned by the result. Her designs are beautiful and spiritual and are inspired by a deep love for what she does and how she connects with the people she works with.

My next chemo is on April 4, and I am actually looking forward to it because it brings me one step closer to putting this cancer behind me. Going through cancer this time is like having a second child. The first time everything is a novelty and you are on hyper alert. The second time is easier because you know what to expect and it is not as daunting.

For my second chemo, you should see what I have planned—a DVD player loaded with my favorite movie, my go-to red-striped blanket, Don Miguel's new book, oranges, and a Cadbury Whole Nut chocolate bar. Oh, and my iPad for writing another blog post.

Midway Checkpoint

May 13, 2016

I am now midway through my chemo treatment for breast cancer: three sessions done, three more to go. I wish I could say that with each chemo, things get easier. The truth is that chemo is not very selective and cannot differentiate between good and bad cells; it just kills everything in its path. Chemo has a cumulative effect, so that each additional chemo is worse than the one before. Typically, I have found that the first ten days of chemo for me are the worst, and then things improve significantly just in time for another cycle.

The past week, however, has been particularly bad. The fatigue has been debilitating. A quick test showed that my hemoglobin count was dropping rapidly as a side effect of the treatment. Two weeks ago, it was 83. This week it is 62. So today I spent the day at the hospital, where I received two units of a blood transfusion.

As always, we respectfully named the bags of blood. We called the first one Massimo (which means the greatest) and we called the second bag Eva (which means life). I said a prayer of thanks to the donors who gave me this gift of life, and then I prayed as each drop of blood entered my body.

So, there are good days and there are bad days.

Some good days bring exceptionally delightful life events—Shayne is coming home tomorrow from Nairobi. And on Tuesday we all fly to

New York to attend Sabrina's graduation.

Other days are really challenging. I am learning that it is okay to be sad when things are difficult, and I take the time to look after myself. Sometimes this means napping. Sometimes it's about asking for help. Sometimes it's saying no to activities. Sometimes it's just about having a good cry. An important lesson is that it is not healthy for me to stay in this state of sadness for long.

My antidote to sadness: having multiple projects to look forward to that will enrich my life and feed my soul. Right now my focus is on being well enough to attend Sabrina's graduation next week.

You Did It!

May 18, 2016

Two years ago, when Sabrina began her masters degree program at Columbia University in New York, I did not know if I would live to witness her graduation. During the hard days of battling cancers, it was the anticipation of seeing her graduate that kept me going.

A few days before my flight to New York, I was at the hospital getting a blood transfusion to boost my severely low hemoglobin count, which was at 62. Even though blood transfusions are full of inherent risk (the blood could be rejected by my body or be contaminated), I was happy to be getting mine—a low hemoglobin count would have prevented me from going to New York.

On the day before the trip, I woke up and noticed a dark red liquid in my PICC line. I panicked. *Could it be blood? Could it be infected? Did I need antibiotics? Would the doctors let me fly?* I did not sleep all night, assuming the worst. I was convinced that the PICC line would need to be removed and re-inserted and wondered if there would be enough time to do this before I left for New York. I rushed to the chemo unit at North York General Hospital to have it checked. The head nurse saw me right away and sensed my panic. *You need to fix this. Nothing will keep me from seeing Sabrina graduate.* The nurse removed the tape securing the line to my skin and examined my arm. I was in luck. The blood was not caused by a malfunction of the line, nor an infection.

Instead, a blister had formed on my arm right beside where the PICC line was inserted and had burst, oozing blood. The nurse cleaned the area, applied a gel to the blister and taped the PICC line back into my arm. *Now nothing would keep me from seeing Sabrina graduate.*

The next day, I woke up before my alarm went off, full of anticipation for our trip. It was going to be a busy day. I had to go to the hospital to check my blood levels one more time before Dr Robson would clear me for travel, while Nagib was presenting at his company's very important annual general meeting. We were planning to meet at the airport at 4 PM sharp to board our flight to New York.

My mind was racing as I waited for my blood work to return from the lab, wondering what would happen if my hemoglobin count had dropped again. *One bag of blood. Two hours for the infusion. Forty-five minutes to get home, change and make it to the airport just in time before the gate closes. But what if the transfusion takes longer?* My phone buzzed. It was Shayne. He had left his favorite blue-striped dress shirt at the dry cleaners and reminded me to pick it up and bring it to New York because "I only have a purple shirt with me and it won't match with my cobalt blue suit." I hissed in frustration. *I don't have the energy to deal with this. My brain is tired. I just need to focus on getting the blood results, driving home, showering, finishing packing and getting to the airport. Wait, was I supposed to meet Nagib at home or at the airport?* Time was moving at hyperspeed.

After a long delay, I finally received my blood results. Miraculously, my hemoglobin had climbed to 106 and I was cleared for travel. *Wait, all of this worrying for nothing; my mind playing mind games.* I was exhilarated and emotionally exhausted at the same time. All I wanted to do was to get to the airport. My nurses told me to be extra careful, to avoid large crowds and get lots of rest. *Didn't they know I was going to New York? The Big Apple? The city that never sleeps?* I rushed home, forgetting to pick up Shayne's shirt on the way. I was supposed to meet Nagib at the airport, but he was instead waiting for me at home when I arrived. I think he could sense the fragile state I was in. I quickly showered, finished packing, and hopped into our car. Rush-hour traffic in Toronto. *There is no way that we are going to make this flight.* We arrived at the airport and ran to the Air Canada desk, but our gate was already closed. I was beyond crying at this point. Thankfully, we managed to book ourselves on a later flight. A few hours later, Nagib and I were in midtown Manhattan pulling up at the Airbnb that Sabrina, Shayne, and Afzal had booked for us. I collapsed into Sabrina's arms with exhaustion. I then turned to Shayne and gave him a big hug. "I hope you guys didn't forget to pick up my favorite dress shirt from the dry cleaners," he said.

It was an incredible scene. Thirty thousand people were packed inside a massive square at the Morningside campus of Columbia University on New York's Upper West Side. Families and friends from across the globe were there to cheer on the grads. Seated in a neat row of chairs on the stage were the president of the university, the deans of different programs, "Uncle Jeff" (the nickname Sabrina and her classmates had given Jeffrey Sachs, the renowned development economist), and other officials. The new graduates, resplendent in their blue gowns and caps, sat in their designated spots. Graduates of each school carried with pride the symbols representing their program. The school of dentistry had giant toothbrushes, the business school had fake $100 bills, the teachers' college had apples, the engineering school had giant inflatable hammers, and the School of International and Public Affairs (SIPA) carried the flags of their home countries.

The atmosphere was charged with anticipation and excitement. A sea of light blue gowns cascaded down from the bleachers on the left and right and filled the space in front of us. It was unlike anything I had ever experienced. Sabrina Natasha Premji, carrying a Canadian flag, was right in the middle of this gathering, graduating from SIPA with a Masters of Public Administration in Development Practice.

Then we got to do it all over again the next day, when 824 SIPA graduates from 79 countries had their school graduation ceremony followed by a reception. When Sabrina's name was called out, she forgot all about poise and decorum and ran across the stage where she was warmly hugged by her program director. We got to be proud parents as a number of faculty told us they had a name for her: Superstar—for the work she did at school and outside the program.

Over the past two years, Sabrina had balanced her education with the social enterprise Kidogo Early Years that she cofounded with her fiancé, Afzal. Her day generally started before 5 AM so she could be in a virtual meeting with Afzal in Kenya. Between classes, she'd hop around the city, speaking at the nonprofit Acumen's partner gathering one day and at the Rockefeller Foundation the next. On weekends, she traveled across the world, presenting at Harvard, judging case competitions in San Francisco, attending conferences in Johannesburg and Beijing, pitching in Paris—and she'd arrive back in New York just in time to write her next exam. Often, Nagib and I couldn't keep track of where our daughter was. If that weren't enough, she had now come home to Toronto to support me whenever she could. I don't think she has slept very much in the past two years.

We celebrated her graduation by going out for dinner and seeing *Aladdin* on Broadway. I wished I could stay a few more days in New York to prolong my euphoria, but we had to return on Friday for blood work to prepare for chemo number four on Tuesday, after the long weekend. I boarded the flight back to Toronto on May 20, my heart full of joy and happiness. *Nothing could have kept me from my daughter's graduation.*

Bitter Lemons

Tuesday, July 5, was a date we had circled on our calendars. It was the scheduled day of my sixth and final chemo for breast cancer and I was looking forward to completing this milestone. Unfortunately, when tested, my hemoglobin and platelet counts had gone down yet again and so Dr Robson wrote up orders for me to have a blood transfusion and asked me to return for the chemo on Friday, July 8.

Alas, it was not to be. Despite two units of blood, my counts were still too low and the doctor decided to cancel the final cycle. His rationale was that my body was taking longer and longer to recover after each chemo and he couldn't, in good faith, put it through yet another grueling round.

I argued vehemently that I should complete my final round of chemo, lest my cancer came back sooner than expected, in which case I would remember this moment and this decision with regret. I also felt fed up with my body. Dr Robson explained patiently that this was the right decision at this time, based on how my body was coping. I should listen to my body and not argue with it. I agreed but felt cheated.

Now my trusted PICC line got dislodged and the surrounding area on my arm became infected. We had been planning to use the line for my Herceptin infusions, a hormone therapy I needed to get every three weeks for the next six months. Dr Robson advised that we should remove the line to avoid further complications. I was disappointed, but not having the PICC line on my arm meant that I could start working out again and so I promptly rejoined GoodLife Fitness. I also wouldn't have to hide the PICC line in photos at Sabrina's upcoming wedding. Trying to make lemonade from bitter lemons.

Our Daughter Got Married Today

July 31, 2016

Today Sabrina married her love Afzal in a beautiful ceremony at the Ismaili Centre, Toronto, where they pledged their love and promise to each other. The reception was held at the Bayview Country Club near our home and they chose a theme to represent their long-distance relationship and extensive travels. The wedding cards were boarding passes, the décor was made of globes and suitcases, the table numbers were countries that Sabrina and Afzal had visited, the food at the reception represented cuisines from all over the world.

When I was diagnosed with breast cancer, Sabrina had called to ask if we should push back the date of her wedding until I was better. If there's anything I've learned through this experience, it's that cancer may be a part of my life, but it doesn't need to consume it. This was evident in the days leading up to her big day, when I refused to let my health stop me from being by my daughter's side. When she came home for spring break in March, we had gone to a trunk sale and found her the perfect wedding dress. The neuropathy in my fingers made it difficult to zip her up or do the buttons, but I was there to see her standing in yards of white lace in the dress of her dreams. She hugged me in tears and asked, "Will you still be alive to watch me get married?" to which I responded "Of course!"

When we were tasting food and wedding cake samples for her

reception, I was too nauseous to try a bite. But I sat beside her as she made her decisions and was thrilled when my taste buds returned to normal for the wedding so that I could taste the food the family had meticulously chosen.

On the first day of the wedding, where we welcome the groom's family to our home and they offer prayers and gifts to the bride, I caught a pesky infection but managed to slip out to see the family physician and start antibiotics just in time to feel better before guests arrived.

As per tradition, Sabrina had henna applied on her arms and legs, a custom to beautify the bride before her big day. She encouraged me to wear a henna crown, and so my friend Tarquin came by to apply the henna and inscribe the words "Happily Ever After" on my bald head to mark the occasion.

Although facilitating workshops for large audiences is what I have done professionally, chemo brain has been difficult to handle and I knew I would have trouble remembering what I wanted to say, so I typed out my speech and read it at the reception.

I was there, wig and all, to see my daughter get married. I said many thank yous to God that day. Thank you for keeping me alive so that I could be a witness to Sabrina and Afzal's love and commitment to each other, and for the promise of Happily Ever After.

Happily Ever After—Sabrina

August 9, 2016

At one point or another, every girl dreams of her wedding day. I could never picture the man or the dress, but there were two things that were always certain in my mind: henna adorning my hands and feet and my mom by my side.

When my mom was diagnosed with her first cancer, we had no idea what the prognosis would be. We were overwhelmed by the febrile neutropenia, the hospital trips, the chemos. There was no space to think about anything except the present. Every once in a while, when I let my mind glimpse towards the future, painful thoughts would surface. *Will my mom get to see the woman I become? Will she see me get married? Will she ever get to become a grandmother?* I had always visualized my mom cuddled up in bed with her grandchildren, reading them storybooks, as she had done with Shayne and me for years. The thought that this might never be would make me tear up.

A guy had stood by my family through the cancers. Though we had been dating for only a few weeks when my mom was first diagnosed, and I was still in Nairobi finishing up assignments, he visited my house often, hugging my mom and bringing her sunflowers. When we had the intensive-care scare, my mom fighting for her life with a dropping hemoglobin count, this fellow stayed with me through the night, as I sobbed in his arms wondering if my mom would make it through the night. He quickly won my heart, and won over my family. So it came as no surprise when on October 2015 he Skyped my parents to ask for my hand in marriage, and proposed to me later that month at the Great Wall of China.

The dreams of a fairy tale wedding and happily-ever-after came to an abrupt halt a few weeks later when I received the call saying that my mom had cancer again. The third one.

For a few years I had been able to lay aside that terrible thought— what if she dies?—and gone back to assuming that she would be with us forever. Now, in an instant, my world had come crashing down again.

"Should we put a pause on the wedding until after the treatment?" I would agonize with myself. "But what if she doesn't make it. Who gets through three cancers and comes out on the other side? Should we quickly tie the knot in a court so she could be there to witness the day?"

I called Mom in tears one afternoon, off-loading all the thoughts on my mind. She vehemently rejected my requests to postpone the wedding, saying she wasn't going to let her cancer get in the way of life. That's who she is. She has never let the illness define her. And from that moment forward, we planned.

During my nine-month engagement, between school in New York and work in Kenya, I was in Toronto for only a few weeks. My mom, in spite of her treatments, worked with my aunt, Zein, to plan the wedding from start to finish. We'd speak on the phone nearly every day during my walks to campus, or in between classes. I found it frustrating at first, and then comical that she never talked about how she was feeling. Instead, she'd want to focus our precious time talking about a potential venue, the guest list, or something else about the wedding.

During some of her chemo appointments, I was able to fly home, and then we would use the six to eight hours at the hospital to go through our list of things to do. She made it a point to tell every nurse who came to check on her that her daughter was getting married, smiling from ear to ear. Sometimes I think she'd forget she was a cancer patient.

I often think back to those days and wonder how she did it. How do you put aside the most important thing that's happening to you and focus on something as trivial as butter cream or fondant on a cake? Especially when you're nauseous. How do you blow-dry your daughter's hair the night before the wedding while singing *Mama Mia* songs when you've got neuropathy in your fingers? How do you put on an "everything is okay" face the morning of the big day when you've caught a nasty infection and need to run to the clinic?

My mom is my hero. She is the strongest, bravest, most inspiring person I know. As I boarded the plane back to Nairobi to begin my life as a married woman, I said a small prayer of gratitude. I got married and my mom was there, right by my side.

Radiation: Cancer's Sunburn

Three weeks ago, on August 8, after enjoying all the wedding festivities and seeing Sabrina, Afzal, and Shayne off to Kenya, I started radiation treatments at the Odette Cancer Centre at Sunnybrook Hospital. The plan was for daily treatments five days a week for five weeks. This was the first time in my cancer history that I was undergoing radiation. The first planning session was long, and I had to lie very still while the technicians determined where exactly they would radiate. There seemed to be a lot of calculations as they moved me, first this way, then that way, to make sure they had the coordinates just right.

There is a significant difference between chemotherapy and radiation. Chemotherapy is not very intelligent or selective. It invades the body and destroys cancer cells as well as perfectly healthy ones, because it just does not know the difference. Radiation, on the other hand, is about precision and it targets only the specific areas where cancerous cells are seen (in my case, the right breast and the lymph nodes under my right arm).

Having experienced bone-marrow aspirations, blood transfusions, and high doses of chemotherapy, I found radiation pleasantly tolerable. My job was to lie still on the bed and let the technicians zap the cancer from a machine outside the room. From time to time, they would come to the room to move me slightly to make sure that the right area got radiated. "Don't do anything; don't try to help me; allow me to move you," was something I heard at every radiation session.

Like the many other treatments I had, the side effects were not seen until a few days later. I am now more than halfway through my radiation treatments, and I'm noticing that I'm more fatigued than usual, and wearing a bra is becoming more and more difficult as the straps cut into my skin and cause bruises. Now I rely on cotton camisoles that are less restrictive but give me some support to my uneven breasts. With each passing radiation session, the pain intensifies—it's like an angry sunburn that doesn't go away. I have been prescribed a water-based cream that I slather on the area a few times a day and I do this diligently.

Overall, I am feeling strong and optimistic. Yet again I see the benefit of focusing on all that is great in my life—family, love, celebration. Cancer is just a tiny footnote.

Daniel, My Brother

October 5, 2016

I first met Daniel and his partner David about a year and a half ago at the Toronto & District Multiple Myeloma Support Group meeting. Daniel had been diagnosed with the disease and he was looking for information on the tandem stem-cell transplant that he was about to receive.

From that first meeting, we became friends. At every subsequent meeting, I would wait expectantly for Daniel and David to walk in the door, knowing that I would be treated with enormous bear hugs, huge smiles, and joyful conversations. We talked about cancer, yes, but cancer did not define our relationship. And that is true of all the individuals I have met at the Myeloma Support Group. It is an eclectic group that includes engineers, businessmen, a pilot, a university professor, government workers, a restaurant owner, investment professionals, retired people, and their caregivers—cancer is not choosy about whom it captures in its web. The connecting bond is that we are all touched by myeloma. The support group is our learning laboratory; a place where we get to hear from renowned doctors and other professionals who share information about treatment options, medication that is still in the pipeline, and managing symptoms. It is also a place for myeloma troopers and caregivers to come together, have conversations, and share stories. A couple of members have been fighting myeloma for eighteen years; they are beacons of hope for the rest of us. Then there are the newbies, who come to the meetings with worry on their faces, just trying to figure things out. And then there are those who stop coming to meetings, too sick to attend. We later learn through their caregivers that they have succumbed to the disease.

Today, Daniel is no more. He lost his fight yesterday and the world is a dimmer place because of it. Daniel had a relapse in late June and his doctors were anxious to start him on chemotherapy again. Further tests revealed that the cancer in his bone marrow had invaded his bloodstream and his liver (this is known as plasma cell leukemia), and that he would have a scant seventy-two hours to live.

Two weeks prior to his passing, Nagib and I had visited David and Daniel at their beautiful condo in the heart of downtown Toronto. Daniel looked weak and tired. The treatment had been wearing him down, yet his spirit was strong and we had a long conversation over tea. We learned that Daniel, a Canadian, was working at a Canadian bank's New York offices. He had been living and working south of Canal Street in lower Manhattan on September 11, 2001. It is an area that received much of the soot and particle debris from the attacks on the twin towers, and it took nearly ten years for the multiple myeloma to surface in Daniel. He is among the thousands who were affected by the toxic and hazardous air that swirled through southern Manhattan. More than fifteen years later, there are over 75,000 patients enrolled in the World Trade Centre Health Program; nearly 23,000 are receiving treatment for conditions such as multiple myeloma. Fifteen years after 9/11, the death toll continues to rise.

The fragility of life. The loss of loved ones. The sadness and pain that cancer can cause. All these things are very real for me as I come to terms with Daniel's death and the loss of other friends through cancer. Daniel reminded me of the gift of friendship, of making each moment count, and of being a good person. This is his legacy that I will always hold on to.

The Spoon Theory

November 7, 2016

Today I woke up full of optimism, ready to tackle the day ahead. I had plans to make a quick breakfast, head to the gym for my aqua fitness class, and rush back in time for a conference call on a project I've been working on. But a few minutes after getting out of bed, I realized that it was going to be a "low spoon" day. Just getting out of bed and brushing my teeth was a huge effort. Two spoons. I decided to take a shower and wash my hair. Two more spoons. It was 9:30 AM and I was exhausted. I canceled my gym class, postponed the conference call, and crawled back into bed.

"Spoon Theory" is a term coined by Christine Miserandino as a visual metaphor to explain what it's like to live with a chronic condition. Most healthy people start the day with many spoons; but when you are chronically ill you only have a limited number of spoons, say twelve, to manage all the things you need to do to get through the day. Each activity—from making breakfast, to getting dressed, to driving to work, to attending meetings—depletes the number of spoons you have. If you use up your twelve spoons, you have to borrow spoons from the next day; then you have fewer spoons to work with the following day and life becomes even more difficult. That is how I feel most days.

The problem with having fewer spoons than you would like is that the world narrows. There is limited time and reduced energy to do everything I want to do, and I have to make careful choices every day on how I spend them. If I write a blog post, I may not have the energy to cook. If I have a doctor's visit, that may tire me out for the rest of the day. Even quieter tasks like reading, watching a baseball game, or listening to a podcast take concentrated energy, and after a few minutes I find myself exhausted, fighting to keep my eyes open.

Pre-cancer, I had an unlimited number of spoons. They came in different colors and sizes. Now the situation is different. One way that I have been able to conserve my spoons is to ask for help. My sense of myself is tied to being self-sufficient and asking for help is anathema for me. At home, on my low-spoon days, I have learned to ask for a cup of tea or a hot water bottle when I am too weak to get it myself. Some days I even keep aside a couple of spoons for later use, when I know I might need them for a project I'm working on or an event I am attending that evening.

The spoon metaphor has now become part of our vocabulary at home. Rather than asking, "How are you?" Nagib, and increasingly my mom, will ask, "How many spoons do you have?" which makes for a more constructive conversation. When a friend asks me how I'm doing, rather than saying, "tired but happy," I just say, "today is a six-spoon kind of day."

Having a limited number of spoons is not all bad. It forces me to make choices about where to put my attention. But every once in a while, I lament that I have limited spoons. Would I want more spoons in my day? Of course I would. I love living in a world of possibilities and having an endless collection of spoons to play with—and sometimes even squander. I would love to reclaim the freedom I once enjoyed, pre-cancer, of doing what I wanted to do, when I wanted to do it. I wish that the smallest of tasks did not tire me out. But I can't live with wishful thinking. I have accepted the fact that some days I will have limited spoons and will need to rest, recharge, and replenish. And when I have lots of spoons, I attack the world with gusto, live big, live unapologetically.

Ups and Downs

"I'm having trouble seeing," I told Nagib when I met him for lunch after facilitating a session for a client. "Everything is hazy and unclear," I said, as I opened and closed my eyes, trying to bring his face into focus. "What do you mean you can't see?" he asked, the lines on his forehead revealing his obvious concern.

We sat in a state of panic until our lunch arrived and my sight returned a few minutes later. We took a deep breath and reflected on how a normal experience resulting from a few nights of working too late had thrust us into such frenzy. Cancer always seems to be lurking in the shadows.

The frenzy returned a couple of days later when I couldn't read the PowerPoint slides at a seminar, and on the drive home, I had difficulty seeing the traffic lights. My eyes felt like they had been rubbed with steel wool. I saw my optometrist, Dr Areef Nurani, immediately, who confirmed I had scratched my cornea, resulting in a severe eye infection. Rubbing your eyes usually doesn't result in loss of sight for most people, but cancer has left my immune system so compromised that even the most innocuous injury can cause serious harm. After two weeks of antibiotics and anti-inflammatory drops, my sight returned back to normal, though Dr Nurani indicated I would eventually need to have cataract surgery, not from aging, but because years of chemo have deteriorated the tissue that makes up my eye's lens.

Cancer has also taken its toll on my mouth. The chemotherapy administered causes dry mouth, mouth sores, infections, gum disease and tooth decay. No matter how good your dental hygiene is, it is nearly inevitable that you will have issues with your mouth. I didn't realize the extent of this when I underwent treatment—when you're diagnosed with an incurable cancer, falling teeth is not the top of your concerns. And yet, it is the side effect that has caused me the most amount of distress.

The first time I lost a tooth, I didn't think too much of it. Now, five broken, damaged, fallen teeth later, I know that my only salvation is to spend dedicated time on mouth hygiene. At some point, I have been advised that I will likely need dentures, which is something I am trying not to think about. I know it may seem vain or even conceited, but this is a depressing thought.

I continue to live in a state of limbo: not a full-on cancer patient and yet to be fully integrated in the world of the "well". I go to the hospital every three weeks for an IV infusion of Herceptin for the breast cancer. In addition, I am booked for an echocardiogram every three months to make sure that my heart is functioning well, since heart-muscle damage is a potential side effect of Herceptin. It's all connected.

Some days I feel that this is what my life is destined to be—regular visits to the hospital, worrying about every new sign and symptom, wondering what comes next. I see my children building and growing their careers in Kenya. I see friends and colleagues moving on and living their lives—becoming grandparents, taking on new jobs, planning to retire, traveling extensively, going back to school. And I feel static. It is almost like I am no longer afflicted with cancer, and yet, my life revolves around the hospital.

On the plus side, I was invited by my surgeon at North York General Hospital, Dr Pinchuk, to participate in a campaign organized by the hospital and Knixwear. Knixwear is an intimate-apparel company and maker of the Evolution Bra, which was created with the guiding principles of "comfortable can be cute" and "functional can be fashionable." The Evolution Bra is anti-odor, quick-dry, fully reversible with a seamless design, and is completely underwire free. Best of all, the fabric completely molds to your unique shape.

The hospital approached Knixwear to design bras that would benefit patients who were going through breast cancer treatment. The campaign featured five women who had undergone breast cancer treatment at North York General. Each of us was asked to choose a word that described her journey with cancer. My colleagues picked Strength, Victory, Transform, and Heart. I chose Resilience. These words are tastefully displayed on the new special edition Evolution Bras, so I now actually have a bra named after me—The Munira Bra! The bra retails for $60, with $30 from each sale going directly to the hospital to help raise $100,000 to buy a new biopsy table for its Breast Diagnostic Centre.

One other piece of really good news is that my multiple myeloma is behaving. I had an appointment recently with Dr Tiedemann, my oncologist at the Princess Margaret Cancer Centre. He said that my myeloma numbers were "too little to be seen." It is these small miracles that give me hope.

So, it's been a month of doctors and hospitals, of ups and downs. I have continued to work on a project-to-project basis and have tried to maintain a positive frame of mind. When I look at my life on balance, I acknowledge that I have been through a lot. I also feel that I need to get myself out of this state of limbo and find a way to come alive again.

Painful Inelegance

December 29, 2016

Every year, since I was twenty-three, I would join a fitness club, promising myself that this was the year that I would focus on health and vitality. And my commitment to fitness would last approximately one month and then I would give up on the goal. I shudder when I think of how much money I have wasted over the years on this endeavor and, upon reflection, realized that the reason I kept giving up is that I was always the worst participant in the class. And nowhere did this express itself more than at the gym. I have always been a dynamic personality—competitive, overachieving, ambitious, impatient. Anything that slowed me down or kept me from getting things done irked me. Waiting in long lines, rambling meetings with no purpose, cumbersome processes—these were things that drove me nuts. Over the past few years, as I grappled with first one, then two, and then three cancers, I noticed a significant shift in my personality. I have been forced by the universe to learn to be more patient, more accepting. And nowhere does this express itself more than at the gym.

In my weekly fitness classes, I'm the participant who raises her left leg when everyone else has raised their right. I'm the participant the instructor will call out most in class because my form is off. I'm the participant who gets sympathetic looks from fellow classmates because they think I don't speak English and can't understand the instructor—I kid you not, I overheard this after a workout one day.

Painful. And that's okay. Because when I work out, I'm happy. I feel every cell in my body awake and alive. I know what it feels like to be too fatigued to get out of bed, so when I have the energy to move, I move, even if it's the wrong arm or the opposite leg. My aqua fitness instructor, Gerry, once commented that I smile from ear-to-ear through the entire workout.

Pre-cancer, it wouldn't have been okay. I wouldn't have handled the embarrassment well. If I knew I could not be the best in class, I would not even bother showing up. I often wonder what I might have been able to do in my past had I not limited myself. Why did the universe have to remind me three times about the fragility of life and to live life fully, before I started to believe that?

But now I have a new resolve. I see the need to work out, eat right and practice mindfulness so that I can be at my very best physically and emotionally and not be a burden on my family and on society. I have become okay with being the worst in my class, no longer comparing myself to others, and not worrying about how others see me. I focus instead on getting a little bit better each time. The new me is going to travel the world, finally learn how to dance and not be scared to drive to unfamiliar places. The new me is going to see Stephen Colbert live in New York, cook lobster, and master Google Maps. I plan to live a bold, unapologetic life, get out of my comfort zone and scare myself with new experiences frequently, without worrying about failure or what others might think.

I think about this every week when I step into the gym. I thank my body for standing strong through all its ordeals; I thank the universe for its unexpected lessons, and then I get moving, painful inelegance and all.

Wisdom from My Future Self

I first learned about the concept of the future self when I was going through my coaching accreditation with the Co-Active Training Institute so I could add personal and business coaching to my repertoire as an HR professional. We went through a visualization exercise where we closed our eyes and transported ourselves ten years into the future. We visualized where we were, what we were doing, who was around us, what we looked like, our states of mind. We connected with our future selves to seek wisdom and insights. It was a profoundly moving and powerful experience for me. Many years later, I feel very connected to my future self and have cultivated a strong relationship with her. For instance, in difficult circumstances, I will ask myself, "What action makes sense today when I think about it ten years out?" and "What advice might my future self give me if she were standing by my side?" The future self is an imagination of your highest and best self. It is a powerful tool within your unconscious mind that you can access at any time to gain insight, perspective, and inspiration.

From a place of vulnerability, I will share with you what stood out for me the first time I saw a future version of me. I saw myself in a home that stood high in altitude. I was noticeably older, with deep laugh lines and short hair. I felt alive and well and completely comfortable in my own skin. And I was at peace, feeling God's presence in every fibre of my being. I was sitting cross-legged on a comfortable sofa with Nagib smiling by my side. The home was filled with people, all talking and laughing, some doing yoga, others resting, all happy to be there. There were colorful rugs and books everywhere, and a guitar was playing. And the food was plentiful—salads and sushi and platters of this and that. The scent was apple cinnamon mixed with warm bread and freesias. And every time the doorbell rang, there was a sense of expectancy about who was joining us. At one point, I went to the door and opened it to see Shayne walk in, wearing a fitted blue sweater, with a special someone with him and two kids at hand. Sabrina and Afzal were right behind them, holding hands, talking excitedly about a new project they were working on. I remember how much my heart was filled with love and gratitude. I asked my future self, "How did we get here?" and she responded with a laugh, "By living our lives fully and fearlessly, by making conscious choices and by having faith." Every time I do my future-self visualization, I find myself returning to that same home; sometimes there are different people around me, sometimes there are different conversations going on; what remains consistent is the sense of utter peace and wellbeing that I am where I need to be.

Channeling my future self, I offer three lessons.

1. Acceptance, Surrender, and God. Cancer is a reminder to us to throw out the notion that we have ultimate control of life. There is only accepting what is here right now, without living in the past or obsessing about the future. This type of acceptance does not mean giving up on life or being a victim of circumstance. It is about daring to let go and trusting the flow of life. It is about respecting where we are at a particular time and participating in what is unfolding, instead of resisting and fighting it. It demands not banging our head on things we cannot control; investing our energy on how we show up and tackle challenges. I'm not always positive about living with cancer; some days I am sad and angry and exhausted. It takes love and compassion to accept myself through these times. It takes courage to accept what I can do and what I can't do given the limitations of my body. Inhaling surrender has taught me to worry less and not sweat over the small stuff. I no longer have the need for control and expect life to do my bidding, so I am rarely disappointed. Instead, I work in harmony with life, understanding that there is a higher force that I am connected with.

My relationship with God has been the single most important factor in confronting and embracing my cancers.

2. Time. Cancer's cold grip forced me to think about how I use time. It is so easy to get caught up in the busyness of life, when, in fact, life is a limited-time offer with an expiry date. The threat of living on borrowed time has made me think about deeper questions. If I had only one year to live, what choices would I make about how I spend my time? Where would I put my attention? What one thing would I want to accomplish? Who would I choose to spend time with? What risks would I take? What challenges would I embrace? When I say yes to something, what am I saying no to? What legacy do I want to leave? Through much reflection, I have concluded that there are only a few things that matter to me: family and close friends, doing meaningful work, serving the community and humanity, becoming stronger and focusing on my spiritual journey.

3. Gratitude. What person have I become on the other side of three cancers? Seven years ago, cancer brought my life to a halt; a plague was invading my body one cell at a time. With the cancer came losses, one after another, and there were days when I collapsed under the weight of this load. But I found that with acceptance and patience, much to my surprise, doors opened for me. Doors to living my purpose and making a difference, doors to meeting extraordinary people, doors to becoming a more compassionate person. That was when I discovered the power of gratitude. I will not go so far as to say that cancer is a gift, because it is not. I would not wish it on anyone. But since getting on this journey, I marvel at my body's ability to withstand three cancers in seven years and come out okay. I am genuinely grateful to be living in Canada, with its publicly funded medical system. I have met extraordinary people who have made a deep impression on me. And I am slowly crossing off items from my bucket list, just as quickly as I am adding to the list. Central to everything is the gratitude I feel towards my family, friends, and community.

A Caregiver's Perspective—Nagib

At one of the annual Journey to Conquer Cancer events that we attended, I was shocked to see a person wearing a t-shirt that proclaimed in big, bold letters "F*CK CANCER." Wow. Our signs were pretty tame in comparison: "I'VE GOT CANCER BUT CANCER AIN'T GOT ME" was one. What could be going through this person's mind, I wondered, to provoke this crude display? Bravado in the face of a daunting foe? Anger and frustration towards an illness that debilitates you so much that all you can do is scream that invective? I soon realized, however, that the angry sign was displayed not by a patient but a caregiver.

With Munira's cancers, my life and the lives of our family have changed in ways that I could never have imagined. Despite all the material about cancer that has been published, there is no manual for caregivers. How do I know what to say, what to do? Sometimes, when Muni is down, all she wants is to be hugged and held. Should I reassure her that everything will be okay when I'm not so sure myself? Sometimes, she wants space—checking her temperature every few hours or asking if she's taken her medicine gets on her nerves. Sometimes, she needs help to do the most basic tasks—like taking a shower; but sometimes, while climbing the stairs, she'll swat away my hand because she feels good enough to do it herself. I get a disheartening and distressing feeling that I have no idea what I'm doing.

Munira's ups and downs impacted me much more than they

apparently did her. I was filled with anguish at seeing her suffer, at the thought of losing her. She on the other hand could brush off a setback and the emotions it wrought and just move on. I couldn't. For the first time in our relationship, I found that we couldn't always communicate with each other, talk things through. I couldn't tell if that was because I was trying too hard to express my concern and care, or whether she just wanted to do things her way. I felt that she was shutting me out when all I wanted was to be there for her. I would brood for a few hours or a day, and things would warm up again between us.

What helped our relationship stay sane was that both of us relied on our key strengths: she is the most positive and hopeful person I know; I focused on the long game, with patience and endurance, until she was well again. We also relied on our faith, our prayers and connection with our immensely generous community, to sustain us through difficult times.

Even though I don't normally curse, I sometimes find myself—particularly on difficult days when there are setbacks or endless delays in getting better—wanting to scream: F*CK CANCER. For inflicting so much pain on the person I love the most. For taking away from the simple pleasures of life—cheering on our favorite teams, watching blockbuster movies on the big screen, participating in community events. For throwing all our plans of growing old together into question. But then I see my stubborn, beautiful wife stare cancer in the face and say "I will survive." And slowly, through her determined resolve to live, I become a believer in choosing hope as the real, and only option.

5.

EPILOGUE

Somewhere in the Mediterranean

May 17, 2017

It's been five years since I was diagnosed with the first of three advanced cancers. Five years of treatment, including chemotherapy, stem-cell transplant, radiation, and surgery. Five years of making hospitals my second home. Five years of ups and downs, agony and exhilaration, struggles and challenges, recovery milestones, and family celebrations. For now, my lymphoma is in remission and my breast cancer has been successfully treated. The myeloma will come back at some point and I will require another stem-cell transplant. But at the moment, everything is stable and I am feeling strong. Nagib and I are celebrating the end of my treatment—and our thirty-fifth wedding anniversary—by sailing the Mediterranean on a cruise ship.

Many things go through my mind. I find myself pouring my thoughts in a journal as I sit alone in my favorite lounge on Deck 4 of the ship, allowing myself to feel deeply the impact of the cancer on my life and letting the tears flow uncontrollably. Cancer came with thorns, with barbed wire, with sharp claws. Cancer makes you vulnerable. It establishes its power over you and takes away your sense of invincibility. You may be the capable professional whom everyone counts on to manage a complicated project or lead a change initiative, but cancer, especially in its bad days, renders you paralyzed, too exhausted even to get out of bed. You cannot take a bath on your own and neuropathy can render you helpless even in managing the simplest of tasks. Meanwhile the chemotherapy has played havoc with your body. And then there is the loss of everything you knew pre-cancer: work, identity, purpose, financial independence. The realization sinks in that you are no longer who you used to be and that you need to rediscover your new normal.

The past five years have been an emotional pendulum, swinging back and forth. We've cried and laughed, pondered and questioned, found anguish and bliss, zigged and zagged our way through life and death, pushed boundaries and found strength. It is not the life adventure I would have remotely imagined for myself, yet there have been hidden treasures along on the way.

Cancer opens you up to appreciating the value of life. When you are in the intensive care unit and the doctors have given up hope that you will make it through the night, you fight to live. When you have been lying in a hospital bed for three weeks after a stem-cell transplant and see all your numbers plummet towards zero, when your raging fever is out of control and you can't stop the nose bleed, you desperately hold on to life. There is nothing like almost losing your life to awaken you to its value.

Cancer has opened me up to vulnerability, to have the courage to be imperfect, to allow others to see me with all the blemishes that the condition unleashes. Pre-cancer, I only allowed people to see what I wanted them to see. Somewhere along the way, I stopped worrying about failing and embraced the freedom to be me, flaws and all.

Cancer has forced me to slow down. Speed was sexy and exciting. But my illnesses have forced me to get in touch with my inner self. I am now in praise of slowness, for living my life rather than rushing through it.

And while I see the value of being in the moment, I am also reconnecting with my past. Cancer has inspired me to travel back to my home town of Moshi, pay a visit to my old home, pop in to see my old schools, see what remains of my family's bakery and Pepsi-Cola factory and spend time at the cemetery where my dad is buried. It has been an uncomfortable, even jarring experience. Today, my past and my present are aligned and a comfortable part of who I am.

Cancer is a reminder of the importance of family, friends, and community. Simply put, you don't do cancer alone. My husband Nagib has been my lifeline as we battled through the cancers together, particularly in the early days. We were not equipped or prepared to deal with this monster that had invaded our lives, and we had to thrash out how we were going to work together and communicate on the same frequency. How could I honor Nagib's need to look after me, while maintaining my independence? How could we maintain some sanity in our lives? Not easy to do when you are stressed to the limit. I am grateful to Nagib for organizing my pill box so that I took the right amount of medications, for checking my temperature multiple times every day for many months, for insisting I rest even when I protested, for opening his arms to me and letting me snuggle right beside him, for taking me shopping for clothes while my body shrunk or grew, for kissing my bald head and making me feel beautiful even when I was retching my gut out in the bathroom in the middle of the night. I still don't know how Nagib put up with me during my Dexa days, when I morphed into an uncontrollable, aggressive, out-of-control maniac.

I am grateful to my mom, my role model. When I was bedridden and had no energy to get up, my mom would climb into my bed and lie next to me, her tiny eighty-five-pound frame holding me while I slept. I would hear her labored asthmatic breathing as she stroked my bald head while holding back her tears. We treasured this time together as we quietly contemplated the fragility of life and the gift of being together in spite of her age and my condition.

I am grateful to my son Shayne. He is my go-to person for conversations, getting perspective, testing new ideas, and working through the good and not-so-good stuff. He is an extraordinary listener and with him, there is no judgment, only understanding. With Shayne, I can be me, with no apologies. My illness caused him to think about life, what was important to him, and how he wanted to live. We now partly live vicariously through Shayne's life—where he balances a meaningful career investing in health care companies across Africa with things he loves to do, such as fitness, cooking and traveling—he recently climbed Mount Kilimanjaro and went gorilla trekking in Rwanda.

I am grateful to my daughter, Sabrina, who moved from Nairobi after learning about my diagnosis to be home by my side. For ten months, Sabrina came with me to every chemo treatment, every clinic visit with the doctor, every blood work appointment, every test that I had to go through. She stayed with me when I was hospitalized and, to the nurses' consternation, always found a way to sneak into bed with me and fall asleep. She was there to help me deal with disappointments and to celebrate the happy moments. She saw me at my best and my worst.

I am thankful for the encouragement and support I have received from the Ismaili community, from Dave and Erika McMullen, Robert McCaw, Patrick Taylor, Jan Wleugel, Don Hunter, and members of the Toronto & District Multiple Myeloma Support Group, and from people around the world who follow my blog. I am grateful to have had friends "hold space" for me over the past five years. To me holding space is about accepting and being there for the other person in support and without judgement. My friends, Shyrose Hasham, Fatima Ladha, Zein Dhanidina, Leila Rahemtulla, JoAnne Langshaw, and Farzana Khimji have done this for me. This is something I will pay forward. I am thankful to Frances Darwin for her spectactular photography and for featuring my cancer story on the big screen.

Cancer has made me appreciate the medical community that deals with life and death every day. The doctors, nurses, researchers, pathologists, radiation therapists, lab technicians, and pharmacists—each one does their part to help the patient go through the valley. I am particularly grateful to my medical team—Drs Tiedemann, Pinchuk, Robson, Franke, and Baghdadlian, who have expertly guided me through this journey. When I was diagnosed with myeloma, there were only a few drugs that were available to patients for this disease. In five years, there have been many advances in the treatment regimen and people live longer as a result. I am thankful that there is new research on multiple myeloma that will hopefully result in a cure. Selfishly, I am praying that this will happen during my lifetime.

Each time I participate in the Princess Margaret Journey to Conquer Cancer event, my heart swells with gratitude to see so many people. Some are undergoing treatment, some are on clinical trials, some are struggling to hang on. I am always struck that for every myeloma patient, there is a sea of family members, friends and caregivers. People who support us and give us more reasons to live. They are the true heroes of our journey, and many of them continue to participate and support the cause despite losing their loved ones to cancer. In the past five years, Munira's Team has raised approximately $70,000. The funds go directly into life-saving treatments for those afflicted with multiple myeloma and other cancers.

As I stand at the edge of the cruise ship, the wind brushing against my patchy, post-chemo hair, I look down at a card that my friend Shyrose gave me early in my cancer journey. The card came with specific instructions: "Do not open this until things get so bad that you are ready to give up." I have gone to that card a dozen times in the past five years. Each time, I've thought to myself, "Things are bad, but they could get worse. I'm still okay." After a five-year journey through the trenches, I bless and release the card—unopened—and drop it into the water with a prayer that I live to see my sixtieth birthday. It's a symbolic way for me to put the past behind me and to start afresh. Almost immediately, I feel every cell in my body dance with joy.

This is a rare picture of me with my dad. When I immigrated from Moshi to Canada, I could only carry so much. This photograph is precious to me.

The wedding pictures of my parents and Nagib and I. My parents married in Mombasa, Kenya shortly after meeting one another for the first time.

Nagib and I chose each other—we bucked tradition, married young, by choice, and even then knew that we wanted to be together for the rest of our lives. Marrying Nagib is the best decision I made in my life.

Though I wasn't sure I was ready to be a mother, when Shayne and Sabrina came into our lives, they brought us so many gifts. I credit them for opening my world to joy, possibility and wonder. Being a mom has been the most important thing I've done in this world.

223

When you are diagnosed with two cancers in two weeks you pray for an oncologist who is in your corner no matter what. Dr Tiedemann was the guy!

In the ambulance on my way to Emergency. The fateful night of rock-bottom hemoglobin counts when I almost died. My family had braced themselves to say goodbye.

Two days later, Dr Cserti visited me and drew a scene from the battlefield inside my bone marrow, showing how my own body's immune system had attacked me.

I'll never be able to fully acknowledge the countless healthcare professionals and volunteers who kept me alive. One of them was Manny Martinez—the "vein whisperer." He gave me a bracelet that read, "Once you choose hope, anything is possible." It was the inspiration for the title of this book.

As I lost my hair through treatment, I alternated between wigs and scarves. The first
time I shaved my head, I immediately put on
a scarf. I remember Nagib coming up to me
and gently removing my scarf. He lifted me
up, held me tight and said, "I love you and
you look beautiful." In that moment it was
hard to hear.

Photo credit: Chris Hughes at A Nerd's World

I had thirteen wigs over the course of my treatments. They allowed me to
play with my identity, have fun, and even get creative with henna designs.
This one, designed by Tarquin Singh, says "When You Choose Hope."

Photo credit: Kenneth Appiah at A Nerd's World

225

Having completed my treatment for non-Hodgkin lymphoma, Dr Tiedemann allowed my body a one-week break. We celebrated by going to St Pete Beach in Florida. I swam and I danced and I ate. I felt alive.

Stem-cell transplant would turn out to be my personal D-Day. Knowing that multiple myeloma is treatable but not curable, this was my shot at getting a few more years on the clock.

Here is Sabrina at my side during breast cancer treatment. I never expected my children to be my caregivers, or at least not this soon.

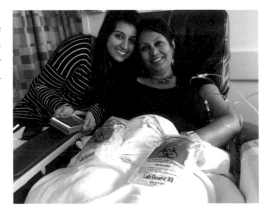

Cancer does not wait for your life's milestones. Here we are at Sabrina's graduation from Columbia University, and at the mehndi ceremony for her wedding.

I was blessed with an opportunity to meet so many extraordinary cancer warriors. Here are two that were particularly special—Pascale Gagne and Tony Gemmiti.

I love these pictures with Nagib and I, my mom and I, and the four of us.